ARTHUR BILLITT'S ABC OF VEGETABLE GROWING

Hamlyn

London · New York · Sydney · Toronto

Acknowledgements

The Editor wishes to thank Banbury
Buildings Ltd. for providing references
for the illustrations on page 19.

Line drawings by Val Biro

First published in 1978 by
The Hamlyn Publishing Group Limited
London · New York · Sydney · Toronto
Astronaut House, Feltham, Middlesex, England

Some material in this book has already
been published in *Amateur Gardening* magazine.

Filmset in England by Filmtype Services Limited, Scarborough
in 11 on 12pt Plantin.
Printed in England by Hazell Watson & Viney Limited,
Aylesbury, Bucks.

ISBN 0 600 39162 0

Contents

General Introduction

The renewed interest in home-grown vegetables comes as a direct result of the ever-increasing price of fresh produce and its lack of flavour. Today so many of the commercially grown varieties are selected for their high yields, appearance and ability to travel well rather than their taste when they reach the housewife's table. In addition the increase in leisure time and the high cost of spending this away from home, has turned more and still more peoples' attention to the rewarding task of growing their own vegetables. The size of the plot is immaterial to the quality of the end product; it is only the quantity that is related to the area of land devoted to vegetables.

For the best results the plot should be in an open sunny position; shade from trees or buildings results in the plants being weak and drawn, which is not conducive to obtaining the maximum yield of the edible parts of the plants. So site your growing area to trap the maximum amount of sunshine available; even if the trees do not actually shade the plot their roots may invade the area and there will be unequal competition for the available moisture and nutrients. I get over this problem by making an annual check for invading roots and cut them off with an axe if they do so.

The initial preparation of the site chosen determines to a great extent the degree of success achieved in the first few seasons. I am never put off by the amount of weeds on a site, the presence of nettles, thistles, docks and even couch grass will tell me that the land has the basic qualities needed to grow vegetables. Unlike most people I make a start on a rough plot by digging all the annual weeds in, roots and all, and have found that November and December are the best months for doing this job. I have given up picking out weed roots as in any case this is never one hundred per cent effective. My experience proves that this is the right treatment on all types of soil, heavy or light, provided the weeds are put underneath and the soil clods left rough on top. The winter frosts, snow, and rains then play their part in improving the physical condition of the soil; this is even more essential on the heavier loams and clay types of land.

In early spring get cracking with surface cultivation, breaking down the spade-size clods before the drying winds take over; the most difficult of soils respond to the treatment (for this I find a three-pronged hand cultivator the best tool). The task of dealing a death blow to the emerging weeds is simple; I rely on the Dutch hoe with which I cut off all weed growth the day it emerges, never allowing it to function as a chlorophyll factory – an essential for continuation of plant life, without which the most vicious weeds quickly succumb. So by May the plot is weed free and from then on the going is easy for both you and the vegetables.

Never resort to re-digging in the spring as it only undoes your pre-Christmas good work; for the perfect seedbed or planting site stick to spring surface cultivations. In other words, successful vegetable growing results from making use of the most suitable site and doing the seasonal jobs at the right time and in the right order.

Arthur's Plot to Allotment

The idea that I should plan and cultivate a 6 m by 3 m (20 ft by 10 ft) vegetable plot at Clack's Farm was first suggested to me by Peter Wood, the Editor of *Amateur Gardening*. My first reaction was that the area was too small to be worthwhile, but how wrong I was! This size vegetable plot could be fitted into most modern gardens which tend to be on the small side, so all who followed the plan, either in their own garden or the fortunes of my plot on BBC 2 'Gardeners' World', know that with only 60 sq m (200 sq ft) of growing space available, it is possible for a family of two to enjoy their own home-grown vegetables for the greater part of the year. Experience with such a limited area has now convinced me that an even more intense cropping scheme is practicable, and during the growing season I was able to introduce 'catch cropping' by sowing two rows of the lettuce Fortune on the spot earmarked for Brussels sprouts (variety Peer Gynt) whilst these were in the seedbed. This resulted in 36 superb well-hearted lettuces, which may be a lot for one sowing but then they did stand in good condition for a long time.

In preparing the plan, I had in mind the need to operate a three-year crop rotation system, so a simple division of the area was made, leaving a small piece at the north end of the plot for the runner beans, with in front of that a limited space for a seedbed and a small herb patch. Having set the demarcation lines it was a question of trying to get a quart into a pint pot. I know from experience that when space is at a premium plants don't understand they should make do with less. To attempt more only results in plenty of weak growth and little edible crop, so I settled for planting distances proved from experience to be right. From then on came the question of what crops to grow. I felt that the variety should be as wide as possible but at the same time each one should be capable of producing an end product in quantity. This meant there could be no place for the less common vegetables (no doubt their lack of cropping ability is one of the reasons why they are not more popular).

Whilst potatoes in years past used to be cheap and easy to obtain I felt that a row of first earlies, to enjoy at a time when they are expensive in the shops, is worth the space – especially if the variety, such as Foremost, has a real new-potato flavour.

The available space determined the choice of Brussels sprouts. Peer Gynt is a dwarf but at the same time a good cropper of quality sprouts. For the same reason the broad bean variety chosen was The Sutton, with Midget being an alternative choice; both are dwarf so don't flop over on to their next door neighbours – often a problem with the taller varieties. Height apart, these dwarf varieties with the smaller beans, but not smaller yield, have a table quality far superior to that of their taller brothers. The same considerations were applied to the choice of a variety for a single row of garden peas, so the early Kelvedon Wonder was selected. A few short canes and some string is all that is needed to support its 45 cm (18 in) of growth.

With each of the other crops the variety chosen was determined by two qualities – flavour and potential yield. It is my contention that home-grown vegetables must always have a better flavour than those bought in the shops; although nothing is nicer than vegetables fresh from the garden whatever the variety.

To those fortunate enough to have a larger area, either within the garden or as an allotment, the cropping can be based on that of 'Arthur's Plot' and the range of crops can be increased.

Always keep in mind the fact that you grow your own vegetables for the kitchen and that you can increase the cropping period of most crops by sowing for succession; any glut that occurs can be frozen.

Arthur's Plot total area = 20ft x 10ft (6m x 3m)

1ft 6in (45cm)	Runner beans Scarlet Emperor. Single row sown in May. Plants on poles 30cm (1ft) apart. Spring onions White Lisbon sown in March.

3ft (1m)	Seed Bed for greens from March-May. Tomatoes Alicante (2) planted in June, followed by broad bean Aquadulce sown in November.	Marrow Green Bush sown April in greenhouse, planted out May-June	Herbs: Mint Sage Thyme Parsley

1ft (30cm)	Carrot Chantenay Red Cored (Favourite) sown in March as 1 row. Followed by onion Express Yellow in August.
1ft (30cm)	Onion sets Stuttgarter Giant planted in March 10cm (4in) apart.
1ft 6in (45cm)	Leek Musselburgh sown in March. Planted out in June 23cm (9in) apart along 1 row.
1ft (30cm)	Parsnip Hollow Crown sown in March as 1 row.
2ft 6in (75cm)	Lettuce Fortune sown in April. Brussels sprouts Peer Gynt sown on seed bed in April. Planted out June to follow Fortune lettuce. Lettuce Webb's Wonderful sown in June between sprouts.
2ft (60cm)	Cabbage Greyhound sown in a seed bed in March. Planted out May. Lettuce Little Gem sown as a follow-on crop.
2ft 3in (63cm)	Potato Foremost sprouted in tray and planted in March. Followed by beetroot Detroit Little Ball, radish French Breakfast, carrot Favourite and cauliflower All The Year Round, sown direct and thinned out.
2ft 3in (63cm)	Peas Kelvedon Wonder sown in March. Followed by radish Cherry Belle and lettuce Winter Density.
2ft (60cm)	Broad bean The Sutton or Midget sown in March as 1 row. Followed by spring cabbage April.

Preparing the Ground

The basic cultivation principles are the same even though soils vary greatly. In my opinion pre-Christmas digging is essential for good vegetable growing. The heavier the soil the more imperative it is to allow the winter elements to play their part, not only in making the land easier to work in the spring but also to open-up and aerate the soil in order that plant roots may spread far and wide with ease. Frost, snow, rain and wind during the winter all play their part in improving the soil texture, especially when the plot has been roughly dug with the clods left unbroken. It is then that the maximum surface area is exposed to nature's winter treatment which does so much to get the land in peak condition for the spring.

Without winter digging I could not get Clack's Farm soil into its easy-to-work condition. If digging is left until Easter it is a totally different proposition. Winter digging affords an opportunity to work in plenty of well-rotted compost or manure – to go on cropping year after year without returning some organic matter to the soil is asking for diminishing yields and lower levels of fertility. Organic matter in the land is necessary for the maintenance of a living soil. Without it the humus content drops and the life within the soil decreases.

Some soils, particularly the lighter types, may need a dressing of lime every three or four years. A simple soil testing outfit can be used to determine whether or not liming is required and how much should be applied: A golden rule is never to overlime, if used in excess vital trace elements are locked up within the soil structure making them unavailable to plants. Under no circumstances should lime be applied to an area where potatoes are to be grown as it always increases the risk of common scab disease.

I find it a cleaner operation to apply the lime when the ground is frozen hard. A day with little or no wind is best, you are then sure of getting the lime where it is wanted, without damage to the soil structure, waste, or risk to you or your clothing.

With the digging all done in good time, the soil will be full of moisture which should be carefully conserved. Spring surface cultivation will do this, whereas spring digging or re-digging allows drying winds to extract much of the moisture, making seedbed tilths difficult to obtain and the consequences of a dry spring far more serious for plants generally.

My advise is: use the spade well in the winter, then put it away after an anti-rust spray treatment; in the spring make full use of a three-pronged cultivator and a Dutch hoe, these two are my best friends for keeping the vegetable plots in good condition throughout the growing season.

Broadcasting lime onto frozen ground

Crop Rotation

Crop rotation is designed to keep the vegetable plot free from serious soil-borne pests and diseases. Most cropping plans are so arranged that no one group of vegetables is grown on the same area of the plot more than once in three years. To achieve this I divide the vegetables roughly into three groups: brassicas (Brussels sprouts, cabbages, etc.), root crops (onions, carrots, parsnips, etc.) and potatoes plus legumes (peas, beans, etc.). Whilst this arrangement is not ideal, it is practical when the quantity of potatoes grown is limited to one or two rows.

No two groups of plants take up nutrients in exactly the same ratio, nor do they excrete the same wastes, a factor little understood. The more serious soil pests and diseases are related to individual groups of plants and do not attack vegetables in another group. For instance potato eelworm is only a problem of potatoes and tomatoes, and clubroot is a disease peculiar to members of the brassica family.

By strictly observing a crop rotation plan the soil is not subjected to a continuous demand for exactly the same nutrient ratios or to the build-up of the same excreta wastes, a situation which sooner or later results in what is known as 'soil sickness'.

Crop rotation denies the more serious soil pests and diseases the continuity build up which can occur when the same crops are grown year after year on the same piece of land. Without the host plants to feed upon, the build-up is either halted or reduced. The idea behind crop rotation is never to give the enemies a chance to establish or build up.

To operate a crop rotation plan it is necessary first to divide the area allocated to vegetable growing into roughly three equal-sized areas. I start by making a plan on paper for year one, in which in section A the carrots,

Runner beans

A	root crops (carrots onions parsnips etc.)	brassicas (broccoli cabbage cauliflower etc.)	potatoes legumes (beans peas etc.)	root crops (carrots onions parsnips etc.)
B	brassicas (broccoli cabbage cauliflower etc.)	potatoes legumes (beans peas etc.)	root crops (carrots onions parsnips etc.)	brassicas (broccoli cabbage cauliflower etc.)
C	potatoes legumes (beans peas etc.)	root crops (carrots onions parsnips etc.)	brassicas (broccoli cabbage cauliflower etc.)	potatoes legumes (beans peas etc.)
	Year 1	Year 2	Year 3	Year 4

Fertilisers and Compost

In the vegetable garden my objectives are clearly defined – quality first, quantity second. Quality, particularly flavour, cannot be obtained unless the variety grown has a naturally built-in flavour. Quality can also be affected by the conditions under which the plants are grown. Therefore not only should each variety be chosen carefully, but the nutrient supply throughout the growing season should be such that the plants can maximise their yield and have the highest level of what I describe as flavour. I regard fertilisers as nutrient supplements additional to those occurring naturally in the soil or to those added by way of well-rotted compost or manure. Used in this way they are a great aid to vegetable growing and do no harm either to the soil or to the people who consume the produce. As has been mentioned previously, continued vegetable growing without returning decaying organic matter to the soil, usually results in disappointments in the long-term.

onions, parsnips, etc. will be grown, section B is allocated to brassicas, and section C to peas, beans and the limited potato crop. The following season, year two, section A will be for brassicas, B for beans and C for carrots, onions, parsnips. Then in year three, section A will be used for peas, beans, and potatoes, section B for carrots and other root crops and section C for brassicas. The following season, year four, it is back to the cropping plan as for year one.

Runner beans I exclude from the cropping plan as far as rotation is concerned, the ultimate height of the row with the shade it creates determines that it shall be at the north end of the plot each year. I endeavour to overcome the soil-sickness risk by opening up a trench each autumn and then allowing the soil to weather before placing some well-rotted compost at the bottom and refilling it.

Both crop rotation and good gardening are needed to keep out such serious problems as clubroot on brassicas and potato eelworm. Make a point of growing your own brassica plants; avoid using plants grown elsewhere as a single infected plant can introduce what years of endeavour will seldom get rid of. Potato eelworm cysts are occasionally brought into a clean vegetable garden on seed potatoes, so it is a wise precaution to wash all seed potatoes in clean cold water before boxing for sprouting. The cysts are easily washed off; better to be safe than sorry.

The Role of Soil Organisms

In the absence of organic matter the soil bacteria populations decrease rapidly. It is these bacteria that operate the soil chemistry mechanisms breaking down and converting chemicals into nutrients the plant can take up. The most economical method of growing vegetables is to make the fullest possible use of these bacteria.

In a garden with a properly maintained soil these organisms deal with the nutrients applied as fertilisers. They work continuously, never failing to do just what the plants appreciate, converting the man-made nutrients into soluble plant foods that can easily be taken up.

To maximise the life and activity of the bacteria, the land must be well drained. They will drown in waterlogged conditions. Heavily compacted soil is also detrimental to them for they need not only the organic matter to live on but also the oxygen in the air spaces within the soil mass.

Soil fungi are not all beneficial but the harmful ones present few problems if the land is well managed. Beneficial fungi will be there in force when well-rotted manure and compost are present. A classic example are the predaceous fungi which feed on potato eelworm, a serious pest if allowed entry to a vegetable plot with depleted humus reserves. These fungi develop masses of minute thread-like loops in which they trap eelworms and digest them. So not only is well-rotted compost or manure essential for high yields but it also acts as an insurance against potato eelworm damage.

Artificial Fertilisers

Although fertilisers are sometimes called 'artificial' because they are man-made, all the elements they supply are usually found in the soil but seldom in sufficient quantities for maximum crop yields. The essential elements are **nitrogen** (N), **phosphorus** (P) and potash or **potassium** (K). These are available either separately or combined together in what is called a 'balanced fertiliser' such as Growmore.

The Growmore fertiliser formula was designed for vegetable growing and is still one of the best for my needs. Nitrogen is the essential element for growth. In Growmore it is present in a form which is readily soluble and so quickly taken up by plants. Phosphorus is needed by plants for root development and, in particular, for seed production. The more proficient the root system, the better use the plant makes of the available nutrients. This keeps the plant growing longer, either before seed production starts or during it, as in the case of runner beans. Potash is the vital health element. When supplies in the soil are at a low ebb, physiological disorders and diseases are more likely. In addition, potash has a considerable bearing on quality, especially flavour. It cannot put quality of flavour into a poor variety but it can improve a good one. It is with these qualities in mind that I always recommend a high potash fertiliser formulation for tomatoes, either in dry or liquid form.

Fertilisers supplying a single element only must be used with great care. In inexperienced hands they are liable to result in an unbalanced nutrient diet for the plants. Consequently, I would recommend Growmore for general use, with perhaps a nitrogen-only fertiliser for topdressing brassicas if they are in need of a growth tonic.

I give my first application of Growmore in the early spring before either sowing or planting. To give the best results I rake it into the topsoil. Follow carefully the rates of application recommended on the label or accompanying leaflet. Any topdressing (further applications made during the growing season) should be applied with care so that none of the fertiliser makes direct contact with the foliage, otherwise leaf scorch may occur. I always lightly hoe in a topdressing and water it in if the weather is dry.

Organic Fertilisers

In addition to the 'artificials', such as Growmore, there are balanced fertilisers based either solely or in part on ingredients of organic origin. These organic fertilisers such as hoof and horn, meat and bone, fish, and dried seaweed are of considerable value. However they are very expensive for use in ordinary vegetable production. Their main advantage is that they have a longer lasting effect.

Liquid Fertilisers

Balanced liquid fertilisers are sometimes more convenient and in certain cases more suitable, for instance in the greenhouse where the nutrient ratios are varied to suit particular plants such as tomatoes.

Foliar feeding, in my opinion, is a technique to be employed when plants are showing signs of some deficiency and need an emergency treatment to get them back into a healthy growing condition as soon as possible. Urea is usually a principal ingredient, this is rapidly taken up by the leaves and gives a growth response correcting any nitrogen shortage. This is also an easy way of supplying trace elements. Deficiencies of these particular elements are often difficult to supply as such minute amounts are needed. Other elements may not be absorbed by the foliage but they may be taken up by the roots and used to advantage by the plant.

The secret of applying liquid fertilisers is to do so little and often. Always dilute the solution according to the manufacturer's instructions. Some gardeners make up their own liquid fertilisers by producing a dilute brew of natural manures such as sheep or poultry droppings. These brews are economical and in the hands of experienced gardeners can produce wonderful results, in spite of the fact that they are in no sense of the word a balanced plant food.

The Compost Heap

At Clack's Farm there are no sources of animal manure so I have to rely on my own compost heaps to maintain soil fertility. Every scrap of non-woody vegetable material is composted. I always have two 1·5-m-square (5-ft-square) slatted wooden bins in use and build up layers of vegetable waste 15 cm (6 in) thick. As I go, I sprinkle a handful of either hydrated lime or garden soil over alternate layers. The lime keeps the decaying mass sweet and the garden soil provides bacteria which multiply rapidly and join in the breakdown processes. Personally I do not use special additives to hasten the operation, nor do I find it necessary to turn the compost or protect it with a sack or sheet from the weather. My bin started in January was three quarters full of superb, sweet-smelling compost by July. When I open up a bin I always take off the top layer of partially broken down material to start the next compost heap.

It is not necessary to have elaborate containers for making compost: a circle, 1·25 m (4 ft) in diameter, of chicken wire kept upright by four strong canes will suffice. All that is really needed is an open earth bottom so earthworms may enter to play their part in the breakdown process, and adequate access for air, so a friable compost is created rather than a soggy mess. The use of well-rotted compost can only do good on any type of soil. The fact that it is well-rotted means that there was sufficient nitrogen present for the soil bacteria to do their job, the added lime helping indirectly in this process.

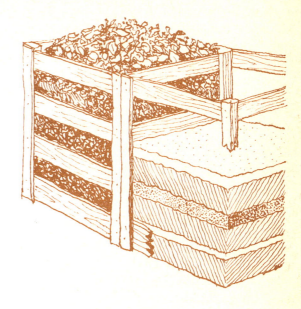

Top Slatted-wooden compost bins, showing how the layers are built up

Bottom Cylindrical compost bin made of chicken wire

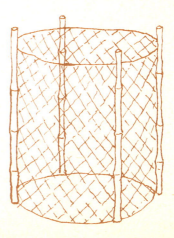

Green Manuring

The application of partially-rotted green material can lead to a nitrogen deficiency in the soil. This can result in a check to plant growth as the soil bacteria are forced to acquire nitrogen from the soil to assist in completing the break-down processes. Green manuring was once a common practice for maintaining soil fertility. This involved sowing seed of fast-growing green-bulk-producing plants such as lupins and white mustard. The seed was broadcast in late summer on land recently cleared of early-maturing crops. Then in the autumn, before the frosts started, any crops still growing were turned over with a spade. This is still a worthwhile practice and provided an application of a nitrogenous fertiliser, such as sulphate of ammonia, is applied overall before the digging operation, green manuring can do nothing but good. An application of 30 g per square metre (1 oz per square yard) of sulphate of ammonia would supply sufficient nitrogen to avoid the risk of any check to the growth of vegetable crops in the following season.

Seed Sowing and Transplanting

Seed sowing is at the beginning of the vegetable-growing story and much depends on how well it is done. The vegetable seed trade is required by law to comply with the statutory percentage seed germination levels. This ensures that when the gardener purchases vegetable seeds they will germinate well and succeed if given the right environment.

Temperature and moisture levels of the growing medium, whether it be in a seed pan or in the open ground outside, determine how long the seed will take to germinate, also how good the germination will be. Another often forgotten factor is the depth of sowing. Small seeds may fail to germinate if they are sown too deeply, in fact they can stay dormant patiently waiting for the time when they will be brought nearer to the surface by a subsequent hoeing. A rough guide is to sow the seeds at a depth equal to twice their diameter.

Sowing in the Greenhouse

Timing of sowing is important, especially in the greenhouse early in the season. A propagating frame electrically heated and thermostatically controlled makes the germination of tomato, cucumber, melon seed, etc., relatively easy and not too expensive with regard to heating costs. The next stage comes when the seedlings have to be pricked out and need both good light and a temperature of about 16°C (60°F). The same situation has to be faced if the seeds have been germinated in an airing cupboard, here a seed pan completely covered with a plastic bag makes a good germination chamber.

Germination of tomato seed, for instance, takes only a few days in a temperature of 18°C (65°F), and the seedlings should be pricked out whilst still in the cotyledon stage before the true leaves appear. It will be roughly six weeks from seed sowing to the time when tomato plants in 8-cm (3-in) pots will be itching to be planted, so for a cold greenhouse planting first week in May, mid-March sowing would be about right; whereas for outdoor planting in the first week in June it would be better to wait until the middle of April before sowing. No plants are improved by an overlong wait in a seed box or pot; once the growing processes are slowed down, the plants take an appreciable time to get going again and any loss of growing time reduces the crop yield.

For seed sowing indoors I use a peat-based seed compost, that is one with a low level of added fertilisers. Transplanting seedlings from a peat-based compost is a simple opera-

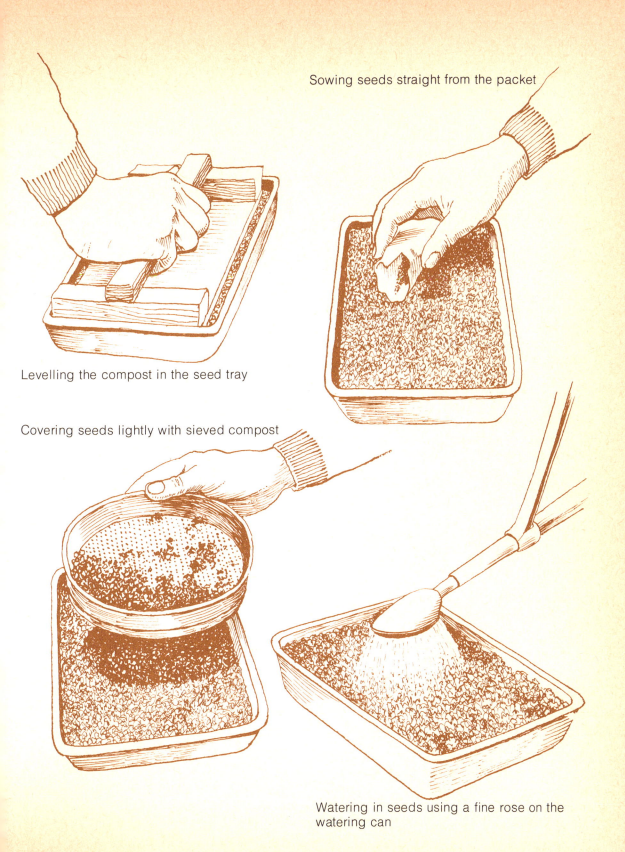

Sowing seeds straight from the packet

Levelling the compost in the seed tray

Covering seeds lightly with sieved compost

Watering in seeds using a fine rose on the watering can

tion, the smallest seedling lifted out carefully with a label or knife will carry sufficient compost on its roots to ensure that it does not suffer a check as a result of the disturbance. John Innes Seed Compost is also excellent for seed raising but its extra weight could be a disadvantage. Use either one or the other; trying to cope with the two types of compost at the same time can be tricky as the watering requirements are so very different. Peat-based composts are difficult to re-wet once they have been allowed to dry out, although wetting agents have now been added to overcome this problem.

A seed compost should be moist but not too wet before use. If it has been wetted too much, leave it till it is a little drier before sowing. For levelling I use a piece of wood with a handgrip, a round one for seed pans and an oblong one for seed trays. Levelling ensures an even sowing depth for all the seeds. With all types of seeds it is advisable to sow thinly and evenly; this means restricting the number of seeds to a seed pan or seed tray. I never sow more than 30 tomato seeds in a 9-cm (3½-in) pot. In the case of cucumbers and marrows, which do not tolerate root disturbance, I prefer to sow them singly in the centre of 8-cm (3-in) pots. Lightly cover the seed with compost and water-in (using a fine rose on the watering can), then all is ready to transfer to the germination quarters.

For early crops of cauliflowers or cabbages I sow in seed trays in the greenhouse in early March. Then while the seedlings are still small, prick them out into peat-pots filled with potting compost. I aim to have the plants ready, without a growth check, for planting out under cloches early in April. Any growth check to young cauliflower plants usually results in 'buttoning' (premature formation of a small head) of the cauliflowers.

Broad beans can also be brought on for early cropping by sowing in the greenhouse. I sow the seeds singly in small peat-pots and plant out the seedlings in a double row under cloches in early April, making sure that the rims of the peat-pots are below soil level.

For those interested in the large onions, seed sowing starts any time between the end of December and the beginning of February. They need a long growing season so I start them off on the shortest day. After germination they do not need or even benefit from a high temperature. Again the secret is to keep the plants growing steadily avoiding even a slight growth check. I transplant my seedlings into deep seed trays, spacing them about 4 cm (1½ in) apart, or into 9-cm (3½-in) pots; if I want really large bulbs some special ones may go from the 9-cm (3½-in) pots into 13-cm (5-in) pots before being planted outside in April.

Sowing Outdoors

A good seedbed starts with winter digging so the soil can have time to weather. By spring the frost, snow and rains will have played their part in getting the top tilth ready for sowing. Wait for the topsoil to dry out and then start by breaking it up. I use a three-pronged hand cultivator for this job.

Spread the preparation of the seedbed over a period of a few dry days, finally using a rake to get a fine, level surface. Then all should be ready for raking-in the pre-sowing application of Growmore fertiliser. This is, I find,

Drawing out a drill using hoe and garden line

Sow two or three seeds at intervals along the drill

the most effective application of fertiliser of the season. For small seeds I draw out a shallow drill using the corner of a hoe held against a taut garden-line to keep a straight line and also to keep the rows separated all the way along at the same distance from the adjoining rows. If the soil is very dry at the time of sowing, water along the drill using a fine rose to help speedy germination.

I space parsnip and beetroot seeds in the drill, placing two or three seeds at intervals of 20 cm (8 in). Other seeds should be sown as thinly as possible especially carrots, the seeds of which are extra small. I use a rake to cover the seeds, drawing it lengthways along the garden-line, this avoids the risk of moving the seed out of the drill line. Finally, I go along the seed row gently using the rake head to crush any small lumps of soil that remain.

Brassicas

For the brassica seedbed, I apply a light dressing of hydrated lime, instead of Growmore fertiliser. Again, thin seed sowing produces the strongest plants. Once the seedlings are well established in the seedbed I go along the rows applying liquid HCH with a watering can, putting my finger over the spout to produce a limited dribble alongside the seedlings. Immediately after transplanting brassicas into their permanent positions it is a good idea to give them another application of HCH to keep the cabbage root fly maggot at bay. All young brassicas should be well firmed in after transplanting. This prevents 'wind rock' in taller subjects such as Brussels sprouts.

Watering

It is often said that once the art of watering is mastered, the road to successful gardening is easy. This is certainly true in the greenhouse, especially when coupled with other means of preventing crops suffering from drought conditions. Then it can make all the difference between a mediocre and a really good crop.

Watering in the Greenhouse

In the greenhouse overwatering is a greater risk than underwatering, especially early in the year. Too wet a compost can result in root damage. Very few plants tolerate their roots being drowned, even for a few days, whatever the stage of growth. In addition a cold over-wet growing medium will add to the possibility of disease. At all times the amount of water needed to keep a plant healthy must be related to its growth rate and leaf area, the temperature of the greenhouse and the extent of ventilation.

Ventilation is important as plants are always more healthy when the air is circulating within the greenhouse; stagnant air is more to the liking of fungus diseases than to plants. If possible I prefer to use rainwater collected in a waterbutt for seedlings and small plants as it is free from chlorine and other additives found in tap water. However, the waterbutt must be kept clean; a well-fitting cover over the top to keep out the leaves and prevent the water going green is a simple solution. The use of dirty rainwater could lead to the start of 'damping off' diseases even in sterilised compost; in fact, if the spores of any disease are introduced into

15

a sterilised medium the spread is far more rapid and the resulting damage worse than in unsterilised compost. The treatment for damping off in seedlings is to water with a solution of Cheshunt Compound (a specially prepared mixture of copper sulphate and ammonium carbonate).

I still prefer to water seed trays and pots individually. This does involve time but it provides a good opportunity to check each plant and water accordingly. A one-gallon watering can fitted with a fine rose makes watering of seed boxes on a bench easy, and does not carry the risk of disturbing the level of the compost or washing the seeds or seedlings out of place as might well occur with a coarse rose. A smaller can with a thin spout is more suitable for the individual watering of plants in small pots; in either case you have control of the amount of water applied.

In the days of clay pots and soil-based composts a tap on the side of the pot either gave a clear 'drying out' ring or a dull note which indicated that the compost was moist enough. Now with plastic pots and peat composts, I check the top of the compost with the back of my fingers. I know that it is unwise to allow drying out to go too far, re-wetting satisfactorily is not easy as the water tends to run down the sides and out of the drainage holes, rather than wetting the dryish compost.

Capillary matting which is kept moist automatically cuts out the need for individual pot watering and supplies the answer to the problem of the gardener who is away for long periods during the week. The pots stand on the matting and the moisture is taken up by the compost in the pots through the drainage holes. However, this technique does need regular checking as considerable variations within a batch of plants can occur. Personally I would find the rapid growth of green algae on the matting unacceptable to my desire for cleanliness in the greenhouse.

I endeavour to keep one or two cans of water in the greenhouse to ensure that the water used is somewhere near greenhouse temperature; a sudden douche of cold tap water early in the season chills the young plant and may well cause a growth check.

In the warmer sunny days of summer I damp down the centre path of the greenhouse to create a warm humid atmosphere. The best time to do this is at midday, followed by a period with the door closed. This creates just the type of condition for good fruit setting on tomatoes, peppers, etc. and it also acts as a deterrent to the build-up of red spider mite which thrives in a hot dry atmosphere. I make a point of carrying out a routine check on the watering needs first thing in the morning; in hot weather it may be necessary to repeat the rounds with the

Automatic watering using capillary matting

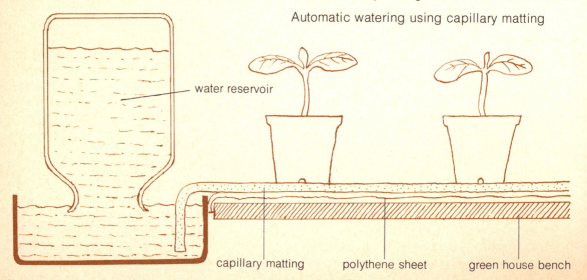

water reservoir

capillary matting   polythene sheet   green house bench

watering can two, or even three, times during the day. In these conditions the chances of over-watering at any one time are slight, but neglect of fruiting tomatoes even for a few hours can result in a crop of fruit disfigured with 'blossom end rot', which shows up as a dark brown sunken patch at the flower end of the tomato.

Cloches
The same basic principles apply to the watering of plants in a cold frame or under cloches. Remember even in the spring the soil can dry out sufficiently to produce drought symptoms, as rain shed by the cloches is usually absorbed by the soil outside the cloches.

From time to time I remove the cloches to give such plants as potatoes, beans, peas and brassicas a thorough watering. I am more careful with lettuces as lateral movement of soil moisture is usually sufficient, especially when the spring weather is on the cool side. In this case watering is liable to be followed by problems with botrytis (grey mould).

Watering Out of Doors
In dry weather seed germination can be improved and speeded up by watering the open seed drill before sowing. Some vegetables are more susceptible to the immediate consequences of drought conditions than

others. Among these I would include runner beans, celery, celeriac, marrows and peas in my priority list for water in time of drought; although if water is freely available, all crops would benefit and give increased yields if watered thoroughly. I make the point *thoroughly* because watering that only wets the soil surface does no more than aggravate the situation. The plants react by developing roots near the soil surface; which usually means their suffering increases as the period of drought continues.

The flower set on runner beans is determined by the amount of moisture available to the roots. These may be well below the 1-m (3-ft) mark so only a very thorough soaking does any real good. The same could be said for all vegetables; one good soak, preferably in the evening, is worth more than many evenings spent damping down the top inch or so of soil with the watering can or hose.

A hose pipe fitted with a cascade sprinkler saves a lot of time which would otherwise be spent holding the hose, also it does water a wide area thoroughly with small droplets akin to rain. A storage reel with a winding handle is a worthwhile investment. It eliminates unnecessary wear to the hose as it is pulled along the path and also keeps it tidy.

Watering when Planting
A simple way to start leek plants on their way is to dribble water into the planting hole; I keep a finger over the can spout to restrict the flow.

My technique for planting brassicas is to have the soil as firm as possible. Plant using a dibber or trowel and firm each plant in well with the heel. Then water into the heel depression with a solution of gamma HCH as a routine deterrent to cabbage root fly.

Conservation of Water
Conservation of the soil moisture is also important. Mulching established plants with well-rotted compost helps but only if it is applied over well-watered soil. However, in the vegetable garden, cultivation techniques are far more important. The routine starts

with winter digging, followed by surface cultivation in the spring. It is unfortunate that many gardeners will wait until Easter before doing the annual turning over of the soil – this is a sure way of wasting moisture stored in the soil after the winter rains. Once the moisture is lost the soil becomes more difficult to work and the young plants struggle to survive until the summer rains start. By then it is too late for them to make up for lost time.

I still believe in the moisture-conserving value of a fine tilth. The Dutch hoe used for weed control also creates a tilth which acts as a barrier between the moist soil underneath and the dry air, thereby acting as a mulch and slowing down the loss of soil moisture. Loss of moisture through the leaves of growing plants during transpiration increases during periods of hot dry weather. Remember this also applies to weeds, so the gardener who maintains a weed-free vegetable plot fares best in dry weather or, for that matter, at all times in my opinion.

Vegetable Growing in Containers

There are few limitations to the possibilities of vegetable growing in containers provided certain basic requirements are met. These are a suitable growing medium, a regular supply of water and nutrients, good drainage and a place in the sun so light conditions are good.

Growing Medium
The growing medium can be either one of the John Innes composts or a peat-based compost. Ordinary garden soil without additives to prevent compaction and to supply extra nutrients would not be very successful. The John Innes composts are a mixture of a sterilised loam, peat and sand plus fertilisers with a little ground chalk.

For most vegetables my choice would be John Innes potting compost No. 2 (J.I.P.2). The peat and sand keep the medium open, allowing water to penetrate easily and, if need be, drain away freely. The numerous air spaces within the compost provide good conditions for root development. However, a good garden soil would do if supplemented with granulated peat and sharp sand (*not* builder's sand). The exact proportions of the mix depend on the soil type, but generally speaking five parts garden soil, three parts peat and two parts coarse sand is satisfactory. Fertilisers must be incorporated and again I follow the J.I.P.2 formula set out below (follow either the metric or imperial)

Metric	Imperial
1 cu m potting compost	1 cu yd potting compost
1 kg finely ground hoof and horn	2 lb finely ground hoof and horn
1 kg superphosphate	2 lb superphosphate
½ kg ground chalk	1 lb ground chalk

This home-made mix will suffice for ordinary vegetables but I would strongly recommend the use of John Innes composts which use sterilised loam for crops which are subject to soil-borne diseases.

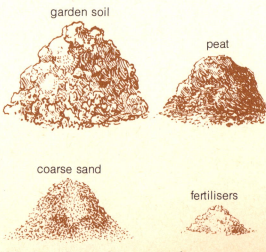

garden soil

peat

coarse sand

fertilisers

John Innes Potting Compost No. 2

Raised bed suitable for a person confined to a wheelchair

A higher raised bed more suited to someone with difficulty in bending

Containers

The size and depth of the containers should be related to the vegetables to be grown. For instance salad crops such as radishes and lettuces would be happy with as little as 15 cm (6 in) of growing medium, whereas carrots, peas, beans or potatoes would need at least double that depth. It is especially important that plants grown in containers have adequate space so thin out seedlings early.

Raised beds. My recent experience with raised beds designed for disabled gardeners working from wheelchairs has proved to me that vegetables grow as well as, or even better than, those grown conventionally. At Clack's Farm we have beds of two different sizes, one for people in wheelchairs and one for people unable to bend down.

These raised beds were filled with ordinary garden soil. The size, depth and construction of the containers ensured that the soil conditions differed little from the rest of the garden. The results with a wide variety of vegetables have been outstanding thanks to the advice of Andrew White, who as the research gardener at the Nuffield Orthopaedic Hospital in Oxford, has contributed so much to the rehabilitation of disabled gardeners.

Growing bags. The most popular version of container growing now is undoubtedly the recently introduced useful growing bags. These are simply heavy-duty plastic bags filled with a peat-plus-fertiliser mixture. These bags are now available in several sizes, the largest being well suited for growing tomatoes, melons, cucumbers, peppers and aubergines; the high value of these crops justifying the initial cost.

Use of these growing bags eliminates the need to sterilise the soil in greenhouse borders. Holes or small slits are made in the sides of the bags to ensure good drainage. Additional feeding will be necessary, in the case of tomatoes the first feed with a high potash fertiliser should be given as soon as the first truss starts to set. Ring culture of tomatoes is a special container-growing technique and is dealt with under the entry on tomatoes later in the book.

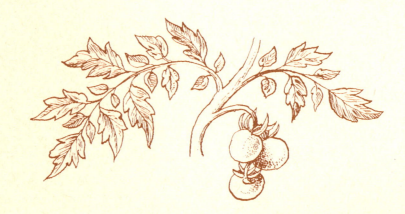

GLOBE ARTICHOKE. This is not extensively grown in this country, although on the Continent it is found in most gardens. Here it is often a question of space in relation to the small amount of edible crop that decides its fate. However, I do grow it at Clack's Farm.

Propagation is generally by taking side suckers from the base of an established plant in March. With a sharp knife go down close to the main stem and cut off the sucker cleanly, making sure that a small piece of root is attached. The new plant will be exactly like its parent. Seed is available but the variation in seedlings is such that I would not recommend raising plants this way.

Cut the heads before the large fleshy scales start to open. After this stage the scales harden, the flower opens and the whole thing becomes ornamental rather than edible.

Give the globe artichoke an open, full-sun position in ground that has been well manured or compost treated. In late February broadcast a general fertiliser and work it in at planting time. The plants will be large. Plant 60 cm (2 ft) apart in rows, or in clumps of three with at least 60 cm (2 ft) between clumps. I find cuttings easy to strike after shading them with newspaper for a few days.

The plants are moisture loving and their heads do not reach full size without sufficient water. In the first season you may only be able to cut one or two heads from each plant, but for the following three or four years five to six from every plant should be possible. The size of the main heads will be increased if the heads on side shoots are removed.

After cropping I cut the artichokes down and clean them up generally – after this they make new growth. In a severe winter some form of protection over the crowns is advisable. Dry straw or bracken would be ideal.

Plant: April
Distance between plants: 60 cm (2 ft)
Distance between rows: 1 m (3 ft)
Harvest: July–October
　　　　　Cut before fleshy scales open

VARIETIES:
Gros Vert de Laon, provides large heads of good quality.

JERUSALEM ARTICHOKE. A tall plant with edible tubers. I used to think it was only worth growing to screen an eyesore, but recent potato scarcities have made me take an interest in the tubers. Contrary to my expectation, when cooked they are not earthy but very pleasant – chestnut-like in flavour and texture.

Jerusalem artichokes are not fussy, and ours crop well in full shade. Before planting the tubers 8 cm (3 in) deep and about 45 cm (18 in) apart in late February or March, I find some well-rotted compost to dig in during winter. Without this treatment the tubers would be fewer and smaller. My original stock of tubers came from a greengrocer's shop. Fortunately they had been freshly lifted – after lifting they dry out rapidly.

When the tops have died down in October I only lift tubers as required for use. Keep aside good quality tubers to provide the material for replanting the following season. If you move your planting site, be sure to remove all the tubers – even the smallest will grow and create a problem.

Plant: February
Planting depth: 8 cm (3 in)
Distance between plants: 45 cm (1½ ft)
Distance between rows: 75 cm (2½ ft)
Harvest: November–March

ASPARAGUS.

ASPARAGUS. This used to be associated only with large gardens but there is no reason why any gardener should not find the limited space required for a single row and grow it successfully.

Patience is all important. After planting, whether the crowns are one, two or three year olds, wait for two seasons before cutting. This is essential if the crowns are to get well established and build up a strong network of roots.

Asparagus is easily grown from seed sown outside in April in a well-prepared seedbed. Sow thinly in a shallow drill, and thin seedlings out to about 15 cm (6 in) apart. The ground must be free from perennial weed roots before you start, and be kept weed free during the growing season – if not the seedlings will be smothered and fail to make sizeable one-year-old crowns. Small packets of the well-known strains Connover's Colossal and Martha Washington are available. Use fresh seed to avoid poor germination.

An advantage can be gained from growing from seed if your patience can stand an extra strain. By allowing the one-year-old plants to stay in a row for another season before transplanting them to the permanent bed, the second season's growth would allow the culling of all-female, seed-bearing plants. The following April the planting of an all-male asparagus bed would be possible. Male plants in general produce the largest spears and without the females around there is no weeding out of unwanted seedlings to be done.

Whether the asparagus is grown in a bed or a single row, once it is established it will, hopefully, go on cropping for 20 years or more. It is therefore most important that the ground be very thoroughly prepared well ahead of planting.

The only double digging I have done at Clack's Farm was for the asparagus bed, working in well-rotted manure at the same time. The bed area had been cultivated for a couple of seasons and perennial weeds were conquered. In the March before planting, I gave the area a dressing of hydrated lime. Asparagus needs calcium much more than the salt so often recommended. When the first gardening books were written, salt was applied to an asparagus bed to control weeds rather than as a response to a need. I never use salt – on some clay soils it could do more harm than good, making the going even more sticky. An application of a general fertiliser is far more beneficial.

I always plant one-year-old, rather than the

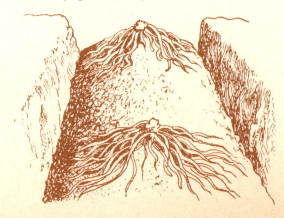

larger two- or three-year-old crowns which, apart from any other consideration, are more expensive. Both my plantings are of the large-spear-bearing strain Regal. Do not allow crowns to dry out. While planting keep the unplanted crowns covered with a damp sack – the sooner they are back in the ground the better. Dried out roots do not recover.

To plant, dig out a trench about 25 cm (10 in) deep and 30 cm (1 ft) wide. Make a sloping ridge in the bottom so that the crowns can be placed with their roots sloping downwards. Cover them carefully with fine soil.

I keep the bed weed free by hand weeding, which incurs no risk of damage to spears just below the surface. Each October when the fern has turned completely yellow I cut it down close to soil level. With the bed cleared I give a topdressing of friable compost and add a layer of good soil on top of that. This gradually raises the level of the bed.

Each season I make two applications of a general fertiliser – one in late February and the other immediately after cutting has finished. The cutting season starts in April and should stop no later than mid-June. Cutting later than this only weakens the crowns and leaves insufficient time for them to build up reserves for the following season's cropping.

Never cut the fern for decoration. The green foliage is essential to the future health of the asparagus.

Sow: April
Plant: April
Planting depth: 15 cm (6 in)
Distance between plants: 38 cm (15 in)
Distance between rows: 45 cm (1½ ft)
Harvest: April–June

VARIETIES:
Connover's Colossal was the most popular variety at one time.
Martha Washington is resistant to asparagus rust disease.
Regal is a strain developed in this country and is my choice for size and quality.

AUBERGINE (EGG PLANT). A semitropical plant which in most seasons will crop successfully in the greenhouse, and in exceptional summers plants outside in sunny borders have succeeded.

I have confined my growing to the greenhouse, sowing the seed in February or early March in the required temperature of 16°C (60°F) which I ensure by using a propagating frame. I prick out the seedlings first into 8-cm (3-in) and finally into 18-cm (7-in) pots, using a peat potting compost.

Spray aubergine with water to deter red spider mite

At 15 cm (6 in) I pinch out the tops to make the plants bushy. Canes and raffia are necessary to support them. When the first flowers have set watering is important – dryness at the roots or too dry an atmosphere in the greenhouse results in a red spider mite problem. If this occurs I spray at seven-day intervals with malathion, which kills the adults. Overhead spraying with clear water also deters red spider mite.

Restrict the number of fruits to five on

each plant at the most to ensure a good size. Until last season I grew Long Purple, but my present choice is an F₁ hybrid Moneymaker, which produces and swells its fruit more freely.

Sow: February or March under glass
Harvest: July–September when fruits are deep purple in colour

VARIETIES:
Moneymaker (F₁ hybrid), an early variety for the greenhouse. Seed sown in February or even January.
Early Long Purple, an old variety, although now superceded by the F₁ hybrids, is still a reliable choice.

BROAD BEANS. From a late autumn or early New Year sowing, broad beans come in ahead of most other vegetables. They always leave the land in a better condition than they found it. The millions of bacteria present in those little white nodules on the roots use the plant's transport system for dealing with nitrogen extracted from the air, and they leave it behind to benefit the following crop.

For the best cropping results the ground should be well cultivated, and manured or compost treated. For an early November sowing this means autumn digging. Broad beans need free calcium in the soil so I always apply a light dressing of hydrated lime when preparing the seedbed.

Basically there are two types of broad beans – Windsor varieties, and the hardier Longpod (Seville) varieties. With both types some varieties are green seeded and others white seeded. There is little difference in flavour or quality but the general preference is for the green-seeded varieties – they show up more attractively in a white sauce.

Aquadulce is good for November sowing. It will stand severe frost conditions without too many plant losses. It is best to sow a double row so that the plants give each other a degree of protection and support.

Dress the seed with a fungicidal seed dressing to protect against soil-borne diseases – at their most offensive when the soil is damp and cold. Make the drills about 5 cm (2 in) deep.

Pinch out the tip of broad beans to stop blackfly building up

For spring sowing there is a wider choice of varieties. Mine would be Exhibition Longpod or Unrivalled Green Windsor. In small gardens one of the dwarf broad beans – Midget or The Sutton – could be a better choice. Dwarf varieties use less space and never flop on to neighbouring vegetable rows. Their crops of slightly smaller beans are delicious. A few canes and a couple of strands of string may be needed to keep taller varieties in place.

Blackfly is the chief enemy of broad beans.

To start with it sets up home in the growing tip, and if this is pinched out the moment the first blackfly is seen a build-up is prevented. If colonies do get going, spray with malathion without delay.

Always pick the beans young, whether for immediate use or for freezing.

Sow: November or February–April
Distance between plants: 23 cm (9 in)
Distance between rows: 60 cm (2 ft)
Harvest: June–August

VARIETIES:

Aquadulce (Giant Seville), a variety for sowing in November or December to provide an early crop in the spring.
Exhibition Longpod, a white-seeded variety, very long pods filled with 7 to 9 beans of good quality.
Masterpiece Green Longpod, a green-seeded variety for early spring sowing, good flavour, suitable for freezing.
Midget, a dwarf variety of excellent flavour.
Promotion, a white-seeded variety, broad pods with 4 to 5 beans, really good flavour.
The Sutton, a dwarf variety, ideal for the small garden. My choice for quality, the beans are small but full of flavour. Sow for succession February to July.
Unrivalled Green Windsor, green seeded, a heavy croppper. Sow between February and April.

DWARF FRENCH BEANS. These are very easy to grow. Outside they crop much earlier than runner beans. Their height – 38–60 cm (15–24 in) – depends on variety. The slender beans should be gathered young while the pods still snap crisply between the fingers – with age they toughen up and will just bend.

When, in a hot summer, runner beans fail to produce a crop, the dwarf French bean crops away merrily, simply because its flowers are under the foliage and away from the intense sunlight.

For a very early crop sow and grow in the greenhouse. The germination and growing temperature needs to be 13°C (55°F) or slightly above for the best results. In these conditions I start in mid-February, sowing one seed per 13-cm (5-in) pot and using a peat-based potting compost with a little extra fertiliser. As the plants develop I give an occasional liquid feed. If it is more convenient to use the greenhouse border, sow in rows 5 cm (2 in) deep with 20 cm (8 in) spacing.

Humidity is important. As the season progresses I water the path and spray overhead with clear water. Under dry, warm conditions watch out for red spider mites. They are minute and may be hidden on the undersides of leaves. If in doubt spray with malathion, getting the spray well under the leaves.

Sowing dwarf French beans too early in cold ground results in indifferent germination – despite seed dressing. For the earliest cropping under cloches it is best to raise the plants in a cold greenhouse or garden frame, sowing the seed singly in small pots and planting out (in our district) in the third week in May.

Remember the plants are extremely frost sensitive. By experience I have learned that here, the first week in June is plenty soon enough for direct sowing outside. By that time the soil has begun to warm up.

I dress the seed with a fungicide before sowing a double row with seeds 5 cm (2 in) deep spaced 25 cm (10 in) apart in the rows with 30 cm (12 in) between rows. I sow a few extras in case of gaps.

Dwarf French beans do best on a well-prepared open site. Just before sowing I rake in an overall application of a general fertiliser to provide plant foods during the growing season. The beans will make their nitrifying contribution to the soil later on, but their own nutritional needs must be satisfied meanwhile. Repeat sowings may be made for a succession of beans throughout the season.

Blackfly can be a pest – again I use malathion which is effective and safe. The varieties I grow are Masterpiece, The Prince, Kinghorn Waxpod – with delicious golden pods and probably our favourite – and Sprite, with round pods of the type so popular in France. Although we do not freeze beans I do know that all these varieties freeze satisfactorily, with Kinghorn Waxpod and Sprite being possibly the most suitable.

Sow: February, under glass
          May to July outside
Distance between plants: 25 cm (10 in)
Distance between rows: 30–60 cm (1–2 ft)
Harvest: June–October

VARIETIES:
The Prince, a well-proven variety, very early, does well under cloches.
Kinghorn Waxpod, a stringless waxpod bean of great quality, pick when still young (15 cm, 6 in, long).
Masterpiece, well-known variety, consistent cropper, good size bean.
Sprite, my favourite, stringless, excellent quality when picked young. Delay sowing until soil starts to warm up.

HARICOT BEAN. For harvesting when ripe and drying, try the heavy-cropping haricot bean Comtesse de Chambord. The pods are shorter than those of the dwarf French bean. They are good picked young for cooking whole but it is more usual to grow them for harvesting when they are ripe as a high protein food that can be preserved easily by drying. In cultivation treat in the same way as dwarf French beans.

RUNNER BEAN. One reason for the popularity of runner beans is their ability to crop from June onwards until frosts cut the plants down in autumn. Few climates in the world suit them better than that of a normal British summer, but when we have continuous heat with high light intensity and little or no rain for weeks, the plants behave as they do in America – flowering without producing.

During winter I open up a 60-cm (2-ft) deep, 90-cm (3-ft) wide trench where the runner beans are to be. In the bottom I put some well-rotted compost – manure would also be fine, and old rags or newspapers would do. What is needed is something to act as a moisture-holding sponge. With a thin covering of soil over the compost I leave the trench open for weathering.

I give the side mounds of soil an application of both hydrated lime and basic slag. On very acid soils runner beans drop their flowers naturally; the lime prevents this. The basic slag gives a slowly-released supply of phosphates and trace elements which are good for any seed-producing plant. About March I fill in the trench, giving the soil time to settle before sowing or planting in May.

An overall application of general fertiliser completes the preparations, without which runner beans on most soils would run out of steam before the end of the season.

For the earliest crop I sow seed singly in 8-cm (3-in) pots in a peat-based compost in my greenhouse towards the end of April. The plants are then ready for planting outside early in May, when cloche protection is needed against frost.

I plant 30 cm (1 ft) apart. When the danger of frost has passed and the cloches are removed I pinch out the growing tip of every extension growth. This foils the climbing habit and keeps the plants bushy. Regular pinching is necessary to deal with new runner growth. Bean formation is at ground level: consequently these ground beans are not all straight – but just as good to eat.

To support the main crop I have either a double row of 2·5 m (8 ft) canes arranged tent-fashion and braced to eliminate sideways movement, or four 2·5 m (8 ft) cane wigwams. A single row of bean poles is all right if it is strong enough to carry the weight of foliage and resist wind. A spacing of 25 cm (10 in) apart gives each plant sufficient room – overcrowding only means a lower yield.

Outdoor sowing dates vary according to district. Here the second week in May is regarded as safe and spring frosts are expected to have finished before the bean seedlings emerge. Northwards it would be wise to wait a while longer. I plant the beans with a trowel, putting a single seed to each support. I put in a few extras as replacements.

When the seedlings start to make extension growths, rather than let them wave about I tie them loosely to the supports with raffia. Later, overhead spraying of the flowers with clear water in the evening is an aid to flower setting. Pick the beans regularly once cropping starts. Even a few beans fully developing their seeds will slow down the rate of cropping.

The one pest to watch for is again blackfly, although it is less troublesome on runner beans than on broad beans. Spray with malathion in the evening when the bees have finished working.

___

Sow: April under glass
     May outside
Sowing depth: 5 cm (2 in)
Distance between plants: 30 cm (1 ft)
Distance between rows: 1·5 m (5 ft) between
                    double rows
Harvest: July–September

VARIETIES:
Achievement, a reliable cropper, long beans of good quality.
Enorma, a long bean, often grown by exhibitors, tends to have a short cropping season.
Prizewinner, a popular variety, useful cropper, good quality.
Streamline, a well-known variety, long beans, tends to have a short cropping season.
Scarlet Emperor, an old variety, free cropper, long season, one of the best for table qualities.
Sunset, a recent introduction, pink flowered, one of the best for flower set, good table qualities.
White Achievement, a white-flowered version of Achievement, which will set its flowers well even in a difficult season.

Supports for runner beans

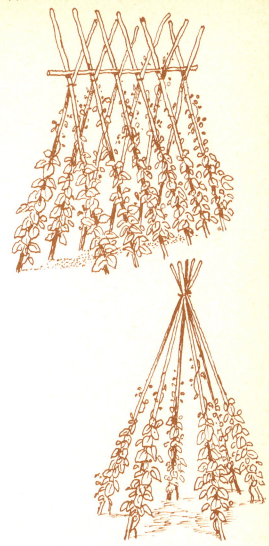

BEETROOT. By successional sowing and winter storage it is possible to have tender beetroots throughout the whole year. Light soils are best but if other types are well worked the crop seldom fails. As with most root crops the ground should not be freshly manured – it is much better for beetroot to follow a crop that enjoyed manuring the previous year.

The middle of April is plenty early enough for the first sowing. For this I use Boltardy, because it is the least likely to bolt to seed when sown in the early months of the year.

Beet produces several seedlings from a single cluster seed so I space the seed singly in a 2·5-cm (1-in) deep drill at 20 cm (8 in) apart. Later I thin out to the strongest seedling at each position.

For a succession of young beetroots I sow at six-week intervals, following Boltardy with Detroit–Little Ball which has an excellent colour. I add short rows of Golden Beet. To retain the contrast of its golden flesh cook it separately from the red varieties.

For the main crop and for winter storage I again sow Detroit–Little Ball in early July. For exhibition sow one of the long varieties such as Cheltenham Green Top in May or June. Beet does not do well in shade. To avoid loss of colour from bleeding, lift the roots and allow the tops to wilt for a few days before twisting them off prior to cooking.

Sow: April–July
Distance between plants: 20 cm (8 in)
Distance between rows: 38 cm (15 in)
Harvest: July–October

VARIETIES:
Boltardy, a variety bred especially to resist 'bolting' (running to seed) when sown in the early spring. Globe shaped, blood-red flesh.
Cheltenham Green Top, a long beetroot of medium size with good dark red colour and good flavour.
Crimson Globe, one of the finest globe beetroots, excellent colour.
Detroit–Little Ball, an ideal choice for successional sowing throughout the season, blood-red flesh.
Golden, a golden-fleshed globe beetroot, good flavour.
Housewife's Choice, a cylindrical beetroot about 15 cm (6 in) long and 5 cm (2 in) in diameter. The right shape for slicing. Blood-red in colour.

LEAF BEET, see Seakale Beet and Spinach Beet.

BRASSICAS

The term 'brassica' is the group name that covers those members of the *Cruciferae* family of plants commonly grown as vegetables – cabbages, cauliflowers, broccoli, Brussels sprouts and kale. Always consider them as a group, as I have done here.

Pests. Brassica pests include cabbage root fly maggot. The fly lays its eggs just below the soil surface on or near the stem of a young plant. After hatching the white maggots feed on the roots, quickly destroying the plant's support system. At planting time I apply bromophos to the planting holes and follow up by watering the plants with a gamma HCH solution diluted to the spraying rate. In addition I have recently reverted to using 15 cm (6 in) plastic discs around stems to prevent the fly laying her eggs close to the stems. The ideal material for this job is roofing felt, but plastic discs cut out of seed compost bags will do as well if weighted down with a stone or two.

Aphids often attack brassicas, the colonies building up on the undersides of leaves. Malathion sprayed directly on to the colonies clears up the problem.

In late summer, leaf-eating caterpillars follow the egg-laying visits of the large and small cabbage white butterflies. The sight of white butterflies is a warning to spray brassicas with either derris or gamma HCH. If the insecticide is on the leaves early, it is ready to deal with emerging caterpillars before they have time to damage the foliage.

Diseases. All are subject to club root, a disease easily introduced into an otherwise clean garden by planting any brassica carrying the infection on its roots. Even soil brought on a spade or boots can introduce the disease.

Crop rotation, liming or fungicidal treatments are of little avail once club root is established. A sprinkling of 4 per cent calomel dust in the planting hole may make cropping possible but does not eliminate the

Using felt discs to protect young brassicas from cabbage root fly

trouble. Liming even at heavy rates is no answer. Dazomet – a chemical soil steriliser – has given good results but requires precise attention to incorporation technique.

The best insurance against club root is to grow your own brassica plants from seed and practise a crop rotation system ensuring that no brassicas are grown on any part of the garden more frequently than once in three years. Bring liming into the rotation, applying it after the preparation of the proposed brassica area.

Feeding. Feeding is important for brassicas – no other vegetables have as great a need for nitrogen. The time to feed is when the plants are well established after transplanting or thinning. I favour a Growmore-type fertiliser, which in addition to nitrogen supplies potash and phosphates for the overall health of the plants.

Transplanting. Don't forget to give the brassicas the benefit of the 'gardener's heel' – they appreciate being planted firmly – this together with planting well down into the soil ensures good anchorage and prevents wind rock.

SPROUTING BROCCOLI. At one time the choice was between purple sprouting, and the less prolific white sprouting broccoli. Now Italian sprouting broccoli or calabrese must be included. Flowering shoots of calabrese, cut while they are still tightly packed, have an asparagus-like flavour – hence the name poor man's asparagus.

Its season is late summer and autumn, whereas purple and white are the winners for cutting in March and April. Sow calabrese in April and treat as Brussels sprouts. Cut the young green shoots before the masses of flower buds swell for opening.

Both purple and white sprouting broccoli should be sown in April or May inside. When the crop is ready the more you cut the more you have. A point to remember is that both purple and white sprouting broccoli stand on the ground roughly 12 months. Plants show signs of frost damage in severe winters but

Firmly plant young brassicas using 'gardener's heel'

29

recover when the weather turns mild. Planting distance at least 75 cm (2½ ft) between plants.

Like all brassicas, broccoli plants need firming in well after planting.

Sow: April–May
Plant: July–August
Distance between plants: 75 cm (2½ ft)
Distance between rows: 75 cm (2½ ft)
Harvest: September–April

VARIETIES:
Purple Sprouting is very hardy so stands well even in a hard winter. It produces its purple-headed shoots in March and April.
Late Purple Sprouting is a late maturing variety which starts cropping in late April and goes on into May.
Improved White Sprouting is a white form which matures in March and April. In my experience it is not as winter hardy as the purple varieties.

BRUSSELS SPROUTS can be cropped over a long season which, by selective plant breeding, has been greatly extended in recent years. However, many of the new varieties have been bred with commercial rather than home growing in mind.

For example, most F_1 hybrids produce sprouts all ready from top to bottom of the stem at the same time, which is fine for machine picking in the field. Speaking for myself, I want sprout picking in the garden to start in October, not July or August as happens with some commercial varieties. I want the sprouts to mature on each stem over a period of a few weeks and so give a continuous supply for the kitchen.

F_1 hybrids that do seem right for our needs are Peer Gynt and Citadel. Peer Gynt is short stemmed and therefore a good choice for a windswept site. It starts our sprout season in October and picked by stages from bottom to top the sprouts stay in good condition for a long time which is quite an advantage.

The same can be said of Citadel, which is rather taller and usually at its best for Christmas. For those who still like a larger sprout, Bedford–Fillbasket is a well-tried variety that can give weight, quality and flavour. To carry the picking season over Christmas and on to March I grow Bedford–Market Rearguard.

Sow Brussels sprouts in shallow drills 1 cm (½ in) deep in March, and thinly so that the plants grow strong and are not drawn. Transplant in rows 1 m (3 ft) apart in May or early June with about 75 cm (2½ ft) between plants.

The ground must be well settled after its winter digging. Plant the sprouts firmly with a dibber, then water each plant with liquid gamma HCH or sprinkle bromophos granules around the stem as protection against cabbage root fly. After the plants are established, apply a small handful of general fertiliser around each plant and hoe in.

Aphids can attack Brussels – as soon as you see any, spray promptly with malathion, particularly the undersides of the leaves. Without this treatment the aphids will even-

Water into heel mark after planting

tually get inside the sprouts. Spray with either liquid derris or liquid gamma HCH the moment cabbage white butterflies are seen in late summer.

Sow: March
Plant: May–June
Distance between plants: 75 cm (2½ ft)
Distance between rows: 1 m (3 ft)
Harvest: October–March

VARIETIES:
Bedford Winter Harvest, a variety for October till March cropping, sprouts are dark green, medium sized.
Citadel (F1 hybrid), a variety I grow for picking from Christmas onwards, rather tall. Sprouts are small to medium, very uniform, dark green, remain in good condition longer than most.
Exhibition, a variety for picking from November onwards, medium-sized sprouts which stay in good condition for a long period.
Bedford–Fillbasket, one of the older varieties, large sprouts, heavy cropper on most soils, October to November.
Peer Gynt (F1 hybrid), an ideal choice for the small plot, dwarf growth habit, ready in October, medium-sized sprouts which fill the stems from top to bottom.
Roodnef–Early Button, an early-cropping variety, small sprouts, dark green, just the type for deep freezing.

CHINESE CABBAGE

CHINESE CABBAGE has several uses. The foliage can be cooked as ordinary cabbage although in cooking it will not smell like cabbage. The ribs of outer leaves are thick and fleshy and cooked separately they are quite different from the leafy parts. The hearts are shredded raw for salad use.

I am coming to terms with this vegetable after two seasons. Being a brassica it is grown in the brassica area so as not to endanger the success of my carefully worked out crop-rotation plan.

July is the best time for sowing. Unlike ordinary cabbage, Chinese cabbage must not be transplanted – simply thinned out in the row to about 30 cm (12 in) apart.

This seemingly close spacing suffices because in growth the plants are more like cos lettuce than cabbage. Transplanting causes bolting to seed – instead of heart and leaf production. In a dry season, water to keep the plants growing and the foliage tender. Well-rotted compost or manure improves the quality of the crop.

Pe-Tsai is the Chinese name under which ordinary Chinese cabbage is sold.

Sow: July
Harvest: August–October

VARIETIES:
Pe-Tsai, pale green in colour producing long, slender hearts.
Sampan (F1 hybrid), has much larger leaves, a solid heart and matures quicker than Pe-Tsai.

SPRING CABBAGE

SPRING CABBAGE. As its name implies, this matures in spring. Most varieties are fairly hardy – in a severe winter the plants may look sad but they improve with the weather.

Spring cabbage is ready when fresh vegetable supplies are low, and conveniently occupies growing space after many brassicas have been cut and the ground cleared. My spring cabbage follows within the current season's brassica area so that the crop rotation rule is unbroken.

In our district I sow in early August. Some gardeners choose late July with the idea that if the autumn is mild and the plants are close planted – 23 cm (9 in) instead of 45 cm (18 in) apart – every other one can be cut as leafy cabbage before Christmas. I do the close planting, but cut my 'in betweens' in March when greens are scarce.

Sow the seed very thinly in a shallow drill. Cabbage root fly is supposed to be less active in August but I take no chances, sprinkling bromophos along the open drill before covering the seed with a fine tilth.

They should be ready for planting out in two months. Do not freshly dig the ground for them. Plant with a dibber and firm with your heel – there is nothing better than the gardener's boot to get a cabbage plant firmly in contact with the soil.

Spring cabbage seed may be sown directly in a row across the plot and thinned out when the plants have got their second pair of leaves. When spring cabbage follows other brassicas I give a little general fertiliser as soon as they have settled down.

Do not give a heavy dose of a straight nitrogenous fertiliser such as sulphate of ammonia – this stimulates excessive growth and can make the plants too lush and too sensitive to frost. Hoe in the fertiliser lightly.

Follow in March with a nitrogenous fertiliser, again lightly hoed in – this tonic will prepare the cabbage for hearting up. The faster the growth the better the cabbage.

April is a high quality pointed variety – smaller than most and therefore ideal for close planting. To follow – and grow larger – there is Offenham–Flower of Spring. This does not mature so early in spring. Before the introduction of April I grew Harbinger (pointed) which is still recommendable as an early spring cabbage.

Sow: July–August
Plant: September
Distance between plants: 45 cm (1½ ft)
Distance between rows: 45 cm (1½ ft)
Harvest: April–June

VARIETIES:
April, a quick-growing, medium-sized pointed cabbage with little or no leaf waste.
Offenham–Flower of Spring, not as early as April or Harbinger but makes a larger heart which stands a long time before cracking.
Harbinger, a small, quality, pointed cabbage which I still grow for its flavour.
Wheeler's Imperial, a pointed cabbage, still a great favourite due to its consistency.

SUMMER CABBAGE. This crop is sown in early spring. It grows in late spring and matures during summer. From start to finish the plants are enjoying conditions that are conducive to quick growth. To be really tender cabbages need to grow quickly without a check.

Remember that summer cabbages come in at the same time as peas, beans, carrots and so on – nevertheless I do not despise cabbage as a fresh vegetable even in the days of plenty.

With the follow-on after spring cabbage in mind I sow June Star in the greenhouse in February. Little heat is required. As soon as the seedlings can be handled I prick them out

After cutting spring cabbage make an X cut on the stem to encourage further leafy growth

in 8-cm (3-in) pots in a peat potting compost for hardening off in a cold frame. In early April I plant them out 60 cm (2 ft) apart.

After they have settled down a Growmore-type fertiliser is sprinkled around each one and hoed in. They make solid round heads by early June. The joy of June Star is that once it has hearted it will stand in first-class condition without breaking for at least a month.

For an early cutting of a similar cabbage, try May Star grown the same way. I have also tried Hispi, an F_1 hybrid pointed cabbage. Whenever it is sown it grows quickly but it cracks within days of maturing and this knocks it off my list.

For the main summer crop sow seed thinly in March or April in shallow drills in the seedbed. If the spring is dry and warm, dust along the top of the drill with derris before the seedlings emerge, as a measure against flea beetle. The planting area should be well settled – not recently dug.

Sprinkle bromophos in the dibber hole and firm around the plant with your heel after planting. Water with liquid gamma HCH against cabbage root fly. When the plants are established I hoe in a Growmore-type fertiliser or Nitrochalk.

I grow Golden Acre, then Winnigstadt which produces a large head. This is an old variety with a good reputation among exhibitors. If, instead of pulling up the root after cutting a cabbage, you make an X-shaped cut in the top of the cut stem, new useable growth of leaves will appear.

For late summer or even early autumn I sow Greyhound – again a proven variety. My last sowing date for Greyhound is mid-July. In most seasons it has turned in some good October cabbages.

Summer cabbage grows through the worst time of the year for cabbage root fly attack. To safeguard against the white maggots that follow the fly's egg-laying, I water the plants with dilute liquid gamma HCH again – about a month after the planting-out treatment. Late in the summer caterpillars can be dealt with by spraying or dusting with derris – a safe insecticide of vegetable origin. This treatment may need to be repeated after heavy rain.

Sow: February under glass
 March–April outside
Plant: April–May
Distance between plants: 60 cm (2 ft)
Distance between rows: 60 cm (2 ft)
Harvest: May–June

VARIETIES:
Earliest, my choice for sowing in the greenhouse in February for planting out under cloches, makes a very solid, tender heart.
Golden Acre–May Express, an early solid round cabbage of excellent flavour.
Greyhound, sow outside from March to June, quick-growing pointed cabbage.
Hispi (F_1 hybrid), pointed cabbage, very fast growing can be planted closer than most varieties, like all F_1 hybrids tends to mature all together after which it cracks quickly. A tender quality cabbage on its day.
June Star (F_1 hybrid), excellent for sowing in February in the greenhouse for planting outside in March–April. A round cabbage of quality, has been my choice for several years, it stands a long time without cracking.
May Star (F_1 hybrid), a ball-headed variety maturing in May.
Winnigstadt, a large pointed cabbage, excellent quality, a variety often seen on the show bench.

RED CABBAGE. A few plants are usually sufficient. When mature the heads are large and solid – a good specimen will turn into a lot of pickled cabbage. If a surplus remains it can be cooked and served in the ordinary way.

Sow in a shallow drill in a seedbed in April. Seed sown thinly produces the strongest plants for putting out in June. Treat just as other brassicas, allowing at least 60 cm (2 ft) between the plants when planting, and follow the usual advice regarding the prevention of root fly maggot.

When established, apply a small handful of general fertiliser to each plant sprinkled around – but clear of – the stem and hoed in. I grow Giant Blood Red which is a very bright red after pickling.

Sow: April
Plant: June
Distance between plants: 60 cm (2 ft)
Distance between rows: 60 cm (2 ft)
Harvest: October–February

VARIETIES:
Giant Blood Red, a large round red cabbage for pickling, also excellent when cooked.

SAVOY AND WINTER CABBAGE.

All within this group are easy to grow, completely winter hardy and a mainstay for winter. By careful selection of varieties it is possible to start cutting as early as August and go on until April – right through the most difficult months.

Best Of All makes a tight solid head as early as August or September. At that time, as well as being a favourite in the kitchen it is often a show winner. To follow in October I grow Selected Drumhead or Autumn Green. For Christmas or thereabouts Winter King or Christmas Drumhead both make excellent heads.

With us, January King is also good at Christmas.

To complete the savoy cabbage season it is difficult to better Rearguard. This is the one for use in March or April. The sowing dates are the same for all the varieties: the cutting season differences are related to the varying rate of maturity.

Sow in the seedbed in 1-cm (½-in) deep drills. With the seed evenly distributed and thinly sown, the seedlings will have room for strong growth.

If the soil is hot and dry just prior to germination and emergence of the seedlings, apply derris dust along the length of the drill to prevent flea beetle damage. The beetles nibble pieces out of the seed leaves, often killing the seedlings.

Transplant into firm settled soil on the brassica plot allowing at least 60 cm (2 ft) between plants. Use a dibber, and firm in with your heel. Water each plant with liquid gamma HCH as a precaution against cabbage root fly maggot – a sprinkling of bromophos around the base of the stem is also useful.

When the plants are established apply a little fertiliser and hoe it into the surface around the plants. Late in the summer, watch for cabbage white butterflies and subsequent caterpillars. Spray with liquid derris or liquid gamma HCH to kill caterpillars.

Sow: March–April
Plant: May–June
Distance between plants: 60 cm (2 ft)
Distance between rows: 60 cm (2 ft)
Harvest: August–April

VARIETIES:
Autumn Green, very dark green in colour. Ready to cut in October and November.
Best Of All, large-headed variety for early cutting.
Christmas Drumhead, produces a good solid head in December.
January King, a valuable late-maturing drumhead cabbage usually at its best in December but will stand well into the New Year.
Rearguard, not the biggest but one of the longest standing varieties.
Selected Drumhead, medium-sized head, maturing early in the season.
Winter King, a long-standing variety, dark green in colour.

SUMMER AND AUTUMN CAULIFLOWER.

From the time cauliflower seed germinates, the plants must continue without a growth check of any sort. Leaving plants in the seedbed too long or allowing them to get pot-bound will result in 'buttoning' – the formation of tiny curds instead of

To protect the cauliflower curd from the light, bend over some of the outer leaves

Exposure to light causes yellowing. Breaking the inside leaves over the curd delays the yellowing but can do nothing to prevent ageing.

For the first summer cauliflowers I sow Classic in March in my greenhouse, prick out into 8-cm (3-in) pots, harden off in the cold frame and guard all the while against a growth check. The first batch go out under cloches in April.

For the main crop, sow from March to May. Sow thinly in shallow drills, not forgetting the preventive treatments for cabbage root fly. When transplanting or thinning out allow 60 cm (2 ft) between plants. The order is firm ground and firm planting.

After midsummer watch for cabbage white butterflies, and spray or dust with derris. I use All The Year Round for successional sowing and cropping – it is very reliable and far less exacting than many of the newer varieties.

For late summer or even autumn cutting I grow another well-tried garden variety: Autumn Giant Veitch's Self Protecting. Its extra large leaves successfully protect its curds from the first frosts.

large ones. Drought or cold after planting will have the same effect.

Cabbage root fly has a preference for cauliflowers so seedbed treatment, followed by preventive treatments after planting out, is essential in most districts. Here, where cabbage root fly is particularly serious, direct drilling and thinning out, plus the preventive treatments, gives good results.

Commercial cauliflower growing is specialised and strictly disciplined regarding sowing dates and so on – F1 hybrids are favoured but in the garden it is hard to comply with the growing specifications. That, and the fact that a row of F1 cauliflowers come in together, reach their peak and pass it within a week or ten days, has sent me back to varieties such as All The Year Round.

A cauliflower curd at its peak is pure white having so far been protected from the light.

Sow: March under glass
March–May outside
Distance between plants: 60 cm (2 ft)
Distance between rows: 60 cm (2 ft)
Harvest: June–November

VARIETIES:

All the Year Round, a variety I always grow, can be sown for succession, very reliable. Large white curds, a favourite with the exhibitor.

Autumn Giant–Veitch's Self Protecting, a variety for sowing in May to crop in October–November, the inner leaves protect the curd against slight autumn frosts.

Classic, my choice for sowing early in the greenhouse for planting out under cloches. Excellent quality.

Dominant, well suited for early sowings either in the greenhouse or outside, large curds of excellent quality.

WINTER CAULIFLOWER. These are the winter cauliflowers produced to perfection in most seasons in Cornwall and the Channel Isles. In mild winters they can crop well with good quality heads in a much wider area.

The varieties grown are reasonably winter hardy but the curds are still sensitive to severe frost – there is always a risk with those maturing January to March in areas other than the South-west.

Sow in shallow drills in April to May for planting out 60 cm (2 ft) apart in June or July. The same care and precautions apply as for summer cauliflower.

I would like to grow Snow–White or Westmarsh Early but to be wise I opt for Walcheren Winter that heads in April or May. By this time the killing frosts are usually over in Worcestershire. Winter cauliflowers stand on the ground for almost 12 months which can create cropping problems on a small vegetable plot.

Sow: April–May
Plant: June–July
Distance between plants: 60 cm (2 ft)
Distance between rows: 60 cm (2 ft)
Harvest: January–May

VARIETIES:
English Winter–Progress, a hardy cauliflower for Northern districts, sow mid-May to stand the winter, ready in May the next year.
Walcheren Winter, a relatively hardy cauliflower for sowing mid-May to stand the winter and crop the following April.

KALE (BORECOLE). This is a rather despised brassica – maybe because recent winters have been less severe than when Cottager's Kale was the universal winter green crop.

Northern gardeners still appreciate its value. I grow one row, from seed sown thinly in a seedbed in April or May. In July sturdy plants are transplanted in a space left by an early-maturing crop such as peas.

Because it would break my crop rotation rules I do not favour the practice, but kale is often planted between maincrop potatoes. In that case the spacing of potato rows must be 84 cm (2 ft 9 in) at least, and the potato variety one with a small haulm growth – Majestic for instance.

I plant my kale 60 cm (2 ft) apart on firm ground within the brassica area. Although cabbage root fly is less troublesome on kale I still water the plants with liquid gamma HCH after firming in.

My choice is Extra Curled Scotch which as well as being good to eat is a beautiful plant to look at in autumn. Pentland Brig is favoured in Scotland, producing leafy shoots in late winter and early spring.

Thousand Headed Kale (plain leaves) is a good substitute for sprouting broccoli and behaves similarly. Feed established plants in the same way as other brassicas.

Sow: April–May
Plant: July
Distance between plants: 60 cm (2 ft)
Distance between rows: 60 cm (2 ft)
Harvest: pick leafy shoots from November to April

VARIETIES:
Pentland Brig, sow April–May, extremely hardy, leafy shoots ready for picking February–April.
Extra Curled Scotch, a variety I always grow, sow April–May for a regular supply of green leaves throughout the winter when other vegetables are in short supply.
Thousand Headed, sow April–May, a plain-leaf kale, supplies plenty of shoots throughout the winter and early spring.

CAPSICUM, see Pepper

CARROTS. These are one of the most useful crops to grow. They are a little less easy for those who garden on heavy clay, or who have not mastered the art of controlling carrot fly – the crop's main pest which is responsible for most of the disappointments and spoils the appearance of the roots.

Carrots are at their best on the lighter soils. On heavy soils the pre-sowing cultivations must be very thorough to ensure that the soil texture is as open as possible. The roots must be able to go straight down without running into a hard pan of unbroken sub-soil.

The best way to meet these requirements on any soil is by pre-Christmas digging – without the addition of any compost or manure. Freshly-incorporated organic matter results in forked carrots instead of straight ones. Ideally in the rotation carrots should follow a crop that had the first call on a well-rotted compost or manure application. A general fertiliser applied when the seedbed is being prepared supplies all the necessary plant foods for a good crop of healthy, well-shaped carrots.

Very early carrots can be grown in a greenhouse border or cold frame. For forcing under glass choose a variety known to respond to the special treatment – Amsterdam Forcing or Early Nantes for example. Carrot fly does not occur under glass and is therefore no problem.

Wherever carrots are to be sown it is impossible to prepare the seedbed too thoroughly. At the time of sowing the top tilth should be fine and reasonably dry on the surface but moist underneath for quick germination.

I keep off the area until the top is dry then the winter-dug soil breaks down easily with the rake the first time through. To get the seedbed just right though, it may need repeated raking over a couple of days after a spell of dry weather.

I wait until the end of March or early April before making the first sowing outside. This sowing is for summer use.

Chantenay Red Cored–Favourite has proved a consistently good cropper at Clack's Farm. The seed drill must be shallow – no more than 1 cm (½ in) deep. The seed is very small (unless pelleted) and great care is needed to avoid the seedlings being overcrowded after germination.

Do sow very thinly – even so to be the required 2·5 cm (1 in) apart the seedlings will have to be thinned out. Bromophos sprinkled along the open seed drill is the first part of the anti-carrot fly treatment. Thin out when the seedlings are about 2·5 cm (1 in) high and water along the row with a solution of gamma HCH after thinning.

Carrot fly is most active during warm weather. The smell of bruised carrot foliage seems to attract it as it goes on its egg-laying missions, so if you have occasion to thin the carrots again repeat the watering with gamma HCH.

Carrots can be sown for succession throughout summer until about the middle of July. I sow our maincrop in June so that it will see us through the winter. On our land I have found it hard to better the stump-rooted Chantenay Red Cored–Favourite.

In autumn instead of lifting and storing either in a clamp or in sand I leave the carrots in the ground, where nature intended they should stay for seed production the following season. I have tried other storage methods only to lose quite a lot of the crop with rots or shrivelling.

An early-sown crop would crack after late summer rains and should always be lifted at maturity on that account. Few cracks occur in the maincrop.

Aphids will attack carrot leaves: the pests are minute but do a considerable amount of damage. I spray them with malathion on sight.

In a dry season carrots appreciate the occasional thorough watering. For the exhibitor with the time to do his carrots really well, a long, pointed variety such as New Red Intermediate or Pride of Denmark could fill the bill. Give them a good depth of soil where the going is easy.

Sow: November–February under glass
March–July outside
Distance between plants: 10 cm (4 in)
Distance between rows: 30 cm (12 in)
Harvest: April–October

VARIETIES:

Amsterdam Forcing, finger-sized, stump-rooted variety, well suited for sowing early in a cold frame or under cloches. Can be sown for succession outside.
Autumn King, large stump-rooted variety, heavy yield when grown as a maincrop for storing. Red cored, a quality carrot.
Chantenay Red Cored–Favourite, stump-rooted maincrop variety which has been my choice for several seasons, it is an all-round quality carrot.
Early Nantes, small, blunt-ended variety, very popular for sowing in cold frames and under cloches.
New Red Intermediate, a long pointed carrot, good colour, stores well for winter use. Often seen on the show bench.
Parisian Rondo, 5-cm (2-in) round variety with a super flavour, a connoisseur's carrot but not a heavy cropper.
Pride of Denmark, intermediate type, smooth skinned, red cored, excellent flavour. A good maincrop carrot.
St Valery, a large tapering carrot, good when grown as a maincrop, more popular with show exhibitors.

CAULIFLOWER, see brassicas

The different shapes of carrots

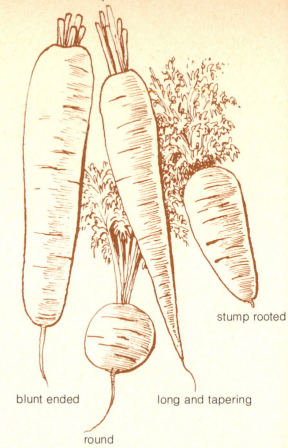

stump rooted

blunt ended

long and tapering

round

CELERIAC. Also called turnip-rooted celery, this is our stand-by for winter soup making. The concentrated flavour is that of top-quality celery. As it is the bulbous root that is used there is no tangle of strings after cooking.

Sow the seed thinly in trays in April in a greenhouse, and cover it with a fine sifting of seed compost. Once more I use a peat compost which is held in the root hairs at pricking out time and prevents a growth check. Germination is best at a temperature of 16–18°C (60–65°F). I achieve this in a propagating frame (fitted with independent top and bottom heating) on a greenhouse bench.

Seedlings are pricked out 5 cm (2 in) apart in a peat compost. During May they are hardened off in a cold frame before planting out in June.

Soil requirements are as for celery – celeriac's near relative. The better and more thorough the pre-planting soil treatment the better the chances of large, long-keeping roots.

Plant celeriac on the level – to do it well plant 30 cm (12 in) apart in a row. Water in a dry summer to maintain growth.

I leave our celeriac in the ground throughout winter, lifting as required. Only on wet, heavy soils would I recommend autumn lifting for storage in clamps or sand. Celery and celeriac may be attacked by celery leaf miner for which a solution of gamma HCH is a useful control – killing the larvae in the leaves.

Sow: April under glass
Plant: June
Distance between plants: 30 cm (12 in)
Distance between rows: 45 cm (18 in)
Harvest: October to February

VARIETIES:
Globus, grown as celery without earthing up, stores well for winter use in soups, starters and salads.

CELERY. Descended from a bog-loving plant which gives a good idea of the growing conditions needed. Plenty of moisture in an open, deeply cultivated soil is the starting point for healthy crisp celery.

The black fen soil of my native Cambridgeshire with its highly organic, slowly decaying peat content was a perfect growing medium. Since leaving the fens I have always tried to develop soil conditions for celery with similar open textures and moisture-holding capacities. I have been reasonably successful on two different types of clay, a light sand and now, at Clack's Farm, a light loam.

For me the traditional trench-grown celery varieties are much better than any of the recently introduced self-blanching types. I grow some of the latter to demonstrate that my opinion is based on fact.

For trenched celery I open up the trench early in the year. I like it to be at least 30 cm (1 ft) deep and a couple of spades wide. If the sub-soil at that depth is poor I would take it out to a depth of 20 cm (8 in) and replace it with fertile topsoil: the sub-soil, used for earthing up later on, would weather during the season.

I work some well-rotted compost into the bottom of the trench to act as a moisture-holding sponge. The trench and side ridges are then left until planting out time. Just prior to planting I rake an application of general fertiliser into the bottom of the trench.

Some varieties are more winter-hardy than others. I think that all celery is improved in flavour by being slightly frosted, but generally speaking the red varieties are the hardiest followed by pink and then white. If I grow one variety only it is Giant Red, but several others, including Giant Pink and

Final earthing up of trench celery

Prizetaker White, have equal crispness and flavour.

I sow thinly in a peat compost, lightly covering the seed before watering with a rose and placing in a propagating frame at 18°C (65°F). Germination takes about a fortnight.

Soon after the seedlings get their first pair of true leaves I prick them out into a peat potting compost allowing 5 cm (2 in) between seedlings. With gradual hardening off they are ready for planting out in the trench in June at 23 cm (9 in) apart.

I prefer a single row but double rows with the same placing give satisfactory results. Coming out of a peat compost the plants carry a good ball of root-filled compost to help them off to a good start.

If the weather is at all dry, water each plant thoroughly throughout the growing season – celery suffers a growth check if it is short of water.

When the plants are about 25 cm (10 in) high I carefully cut out any side shoots at the base before the first earthing up – drawing up loose soil around the plants to exclude light from the stems so that they are blanched white. As the plants grow, they are earthed up repeatedly, until finally they are on a ridge 30 cm (1 ft) or more high. At no time should the growing centre of the plants be covered with soil.

Some gardeners advocate wrapping the plants round with newspaper or corrugated paper before earthing up. This may be good in some situations but in my experience it gives the slugs a more comfortable home. Exhibitors do a good blanching job with drainpipes or long sleeves.

Midway through the growing season the side ridges may be used for lettuces or radishes to save space.

Self-blanching celery is grown on the flat without earthing up. Planting is in square blocks with 23 cm (9 in) between plants. With their own foliage the plants help to improve their natural inclination to blanch. Again, a good, well-cultivated moisture-holding soil is best.

Sow: March under glass
Plant: June
Distance between plants: 23 cm (9 in)
Distance between rows: traditional:
1·25 m (4 ft)
self-blanching:
23 cm (9 in)
Harvest: October–February

VARIETIES:
Traditional
Giant Pink, a variety with excellent qualities both for the table and exhibition.
Giant Red, one of the hardiest, dark red outer stems with blanched centres, if grown well will stand until January.
Giant White, one of the best for table qualities, needs care to produce the heads at their best. Pick October to Christmas.
Prizetaker White, crisp and full of flavour.

Self-blanching
Golden Self-Blanching, very early, ready August onwards, lacks crispness.
American Green, ready in October, stems green, lacks the quality to satisfy my palate.

Use the ridges to grow a crop of lettuce

CHICORY. As a winter salad this is very highly regarded on the Continent. Grown outside from seed, the roots are lifted in November and forced as required for succession. Forcing is done in the dark to ensure that tight bud growth and leaves are completely blanched.

The variety most suitable is Witloof (Brussels Chicory). When grown well it produces a straight, parsnip-like root so, as for most root crops, the ground should be deeply dug. Avoid fresh manuring otherwise the roots are likely to be forked and less suitable for forcing.

I sow early in May and thin out to 20 cm (8 in) apart. Then in October, before the frosts, I lift, trim the tops cleanly to just above the crown and after shortening the roots to about 23 cm (9 in), store in sand in a cool place. With our cellar dark and a constant 10°C (50°F) I know that it will be about four weeks from the time the potted or boxed roots go in to the blanched chicory being ready.

I put three roots to a 25-cm (10-in) pot in damp sand or light soil making sure that the crowns are about 1 cm (½ in) clear of the surface. Keep these in the dark from then on, and see that the sand or soil is always damp.

I have tried Pain de Sucre (Sugar Loaf) which is grown on the Continent as we grow cos lettuce, sowing in July. This unforced chicory with a fairly white, solid heart is ready for direct cutting in autumn, but I find it on the bitter side.

Sow: May–July
Distance between plants: 20 cm (8 in)
Lift to blanch: October
Harvest: November–March

VARIETIES:
Witloof, the well-known variety, sown in May, parsnip-like roots lifted in October for forcing.
Sugar Loaf, sown June–July, grown like a cos lettuce for use in the salad bowl without artificial blanching.

Cutting the blanched chicons

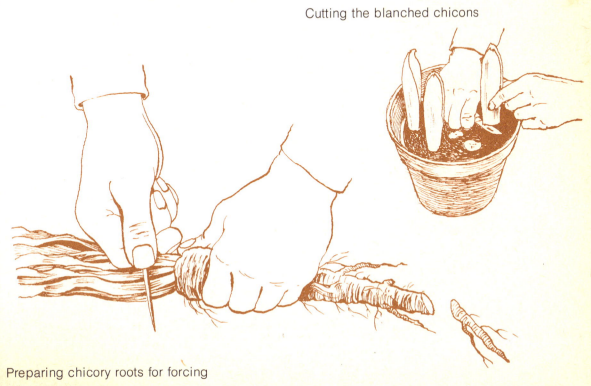

Preparing chicory roots for forcing

CHIVES. These are a perennial member of the onion family. In a very convenient form the foliage adds a pleasant onion flavour to many savoury dishes. Within reason the more the plants are cut during the growing season the better the quality of the thin, onion-like leaves.

I grow chives in the herb garden and also use them for border-edging a small vegetable plot. The purple flowers are decorative for a month or so and if the dead heads are removed promptly the plants do not suffer from their dual role.

Chives are not fussy about soil or position – I have some doing well in full shade. The usual method of propagation is by division of the clumps in spring. The small divisions planted 23 cm (9 in) apart soon increase and may be used for picking later on in the first season. After three years at most I lift, divide and replant, otherwise the size and strength of the foliage decreases due to overcrowding within the clump.

Chives can be grown from seed sown in the open in early summer, thinned out to 23 cm (9 in) apart. In the first season from seed, picking, if any, should be limited. Chives do well in boxes or pots on the windowsill.

CORN SALAD. Also called Lamb's Lettuce and grown on the Continent as a winter salad, is now gaining favour here. Although it can be grown earlier for use in summer salads it is more usual to sow outside in August or September. The young leaves are then in good condition during winter. To keep them that way a covering of straw is advisable.

Last year I tried a row of the Large-Leaved English corn salad, sowing in a shallow drill and thinning out to 10 cm (4 in) apart but I have yet to acquire a taste for this vegetable. Maybe I am spoilt by having winter lettuce on hand.

Sow: August–September
Distance between plants: 10 cm (4 in)
Distance between rows: 15 cm (6 in)
Harvest: when 3 or 4 leaves have formed

VARIETIES:
Large-Leaved English, sow August to September in the open, the young leaves make a good winter salad.

CRESS, see Mustard

COURGETTES, see Marrow

CUCUMBERS. With heating maintained at 18°C (65°F), cucumbers can be grown and cropped in a greenhouse throughout the year, but cost is the limiting factor. I settle for cucumbers in the greenhouse planted in April to crop from June onwards: followed by a cold frame planting in May to crop from July onwards.

There is no point in sowing cucumber seed early unless the right warm, humid conditions can be provided from germination onwards – better to wait and not have chilled plants standing checked, waiting for transplanting in the warmer weather.

For the April planting I sow each seed singly on edge in an 8-cm (3-in) pot in March. The seed is covered with about 50 mm (¼ in) of peat seed compost and watered with a fine rose.

Germination in the propagating frame at 18°C (65°F) takes 4–5 days, during which time I ban further watering. After germination the seedlings in their pots are well spaced out on the bench so that they are never overcrowded.

When strawy horse manure was available I used to stack it for a time to get the initial heat out and then with it cooled and starting to settle, I made a mound of it about 60 cm (2 ft) wide and 38 cm (15 in) high in the greenhouse. There is nothing better for cucumbers, but now that horse manure is out for us – our provider died at a ripe old Clack's-Farm-induced age of 30 a couple of years ago – I use peat growing bags, planting two cucumbers to a bag.

With the bags lengthways about 30 cm (1 ft) from the side of the greenhouse it is not difficult to fix horizontal wires or large-squared plastic netting up to the top of the greenhouse for support.

I do not need a full cucumber house, so while it is true that cucumbers like a more humid atmosphere than tomatoes I grow both in the same house.

After planting I tie the fast-growing main stem loosely to its support with raffia. Laterals (side shoots) soon develop and produce both male and female flowers – unless the variety is of all-female-flower stock.

Female flowers are easily identified by the thickened-stem appearance of the embryo cucumbers immediately behind them. The stalk of the male flower is thin all the way.

The laterals which in time develop along the full length of the main stem should be pinched out two leaves beyond the female flower and tied in for support. Remove male flowers daily to prevent the pollination of female flowers – this results in swollen, inedible cucumbers.

Remove all flowers forming on the main

stem so the crop is borne only on the laterals. The main stem may be stopped at the greenhouse ridge.

I start feeding with a liquid fertiliser about a month after planting out and repeat this fortnightly. Watering is most important. Insufficient water causes wilting, and the cucumbers go soft at the ends in a type of blossom end rot.

With the right humidity and overhead spraying with a fine mist of clear water at midday, red spider mite should not be a problem, but let the house get hot and dry in midsummer and red spider mite will be there, turning the leaves from dark green into dry yellowish shadows.

Bitterness of the cucumber, when it occurs, may be due to allowing pollination, to ageing or feeding with an inorganic fertiliser such as sulphate of ammonia. Some varieties are more liable to bitterness than others. Telegraph Improved has long been my chosen variety both for greenhouse and cold frame.

Growing in a frame. In a cold frame the growing technique is the same except that without heat it is necessary to wait until mid-May or a little later before planting out. This can be an advantage as the later-planted cucumbers produce fruit long after the early crop has finished.

In a cold frame I place the peat growing

bag lengthways at the high end and plant two cucumbers per bag (two per light). The main stem I tie loosely to a laid cane and pinch out the top when it reaches the far end. The rest is as for the heated greenhouse.

In a frame, cucumber foliage grows close to the glass, therefore summer shading – hessian or newspaper will do – is necessary to avoid scorching. During the day I give some ventilation but no more than 2·5 cm (1 in) or so should be necessary.

Sow: March under glass
Plant: April–May
Harvest: June–September

VARIETIES:
Femspot (F₁ hybrid), a variety without male flowers, a prolific cropper, suitable for both greenhouse and cold frame.
Telegraph Improved, a favourite variety for growing either in a greenhouse or a cold frame, excellent quality but needs the male flowers removed.

RIDGE CUCUMBER. Recent variety introductions are far superior to the ridge cucumbers of years ago. The quality comes near to that of the best heated-greenhouse cucumbers. At one time I dismissed ridges as short, thick and prickly, but I now grow a few outside either unprotected or under cloches and also on the floor of a cold greenhouse.

The cropping capacities of Long Green, Baton Vert and Burpless Tasty Green have been outstanding.

I let them scramble about without stopping or pinching out. The occasional liquid feed is important. With keeping the centre path of the greenhouse damped down two or three times a day, the humidity level was such that there was no trouble from red spider mite.

Outside I delay putting the plants out until the end of May. Each plant has a supply of well-rotted compost put down below before planting. Extra watering in dry weather is essential.

Ridge cucumbers growing in open ground

Growing bags are a recommended method for producing a fine crop of cucumbers

Seed is sown in April in a propagating frame, 16°C (60°F) gives good germination. I sow the seed on edge, singly in 8-cm (3-in) pots, using a peat seed compost. The seedlings come out of the propagating frame as soon as the first true leaves appear and eventually have a hardening off period of about a fortnight without heat before being planted out.

Sow: April under glass
Plant: May
Harvest: July–September

VARIETIES:
Baton Vert, slender fruits of superb flavour. Early maturing.
Burpless Tasty Green (F_1 hybrid), a long variety for the cold frame, will succeed in the South, good flavour.
Long Green, a prolific cropper, either in a cold frame or outside, good flavour.

PICKLING CUCUMBERS (GHERKINS).

I grow these outside in a sunny position. Cloche protection, especially just after planting out in late May or early June, gives the plants a good start. I sow in the greenhouse in mid-April using small peat pots and a peat seed compost – one seed on edge to a pot.

As with all cucumbers the germination temperature should be around 16°C (60°F). A gradual hardening off of the plants before planting out is advisable. Some well-rotted compost incorporated in each planting hole makes for plenty of quick-forming gherkins. I grow Prolific and Venlo Pickling.

Sow: April under glass
Plant: May–June
Harvest: July–September

VARIETIES:
Prolific produces gherkins in great numbers and should be picked for pickling whilst still small.
Venlo Pickling grow outside, for pickling, very prolific cropper.

ENDIVE. Maybe the fact that every plant needs blanching before it is fit for use, accounts for endive's lack of popularity. For late summer salads I sow Exquisite Curled in April, sowing very thinly in a shallow drill, later on thinning plants out to 30 cm (12 in) apart. For winter salads I sow Batavian Broad Leaved endive in the same way but in August.

To blanch the foliage cover individual plants with comfortably-sized plant pots to keep the light out, remembering to put a stone over the drainage hole. Alternatively, bunch the outer leaves together and tie with raffia – this only blanches the heart foliage. Blanch a few plants at a time as rotting occurs if they are left in the dark too long.

Sow: April–August
Distance between plants: 30 cm (12 in)
Distance between rows: 30 cm (12 in)
Harvest: August–February

VARIETIES:
Exquisite Curled, sown end of March to July, covered to blanch outer leaves.
Batavian Broad Leaved, sown July onwards, excellent as winter salad or as a cooked vegetable.

GARLIC. This likes a sunny position. My

annual planting is limited to a very few cloves – a little garlic goes a long way with me. Start with single cloves broken apart from a mature bulb either bought or home grown. Single cloves planted with a dibber towards the end of February will each produce a complete garlic bulb by the late summer. This should ripen off before being lifted for storage indoors. Garlic does best in a light soil but tolerates most types.

Plant: February
Distance between plants: 20 cm (8 in)
Harvest: September

KALE, see under Brassicas

KOHL RABI. A brassica, grown not for its leaf, but for its swollen bulbous stem developing just above ground level. It is more popular on the Continent. My first experience was disappointing simply because I let the stem get too old and tough. Gathered when no larger than a tennis ball, still young and tender, it is very acceptable.

Sow in short rows in April to June and thin out to 38 cm (15 in) apart for a succession of

HORSERADISH. This is often regarded as a weed with no particular requirements for its well-being, but if long thick roots are wanted for culinary use it is wise to start with a deep soil trenched to a depth of 60 cm (2 ft). Work some well-rotted compost or manure into the filling-in soil, after planting 8-cm (3-in) long pieces of horseradish root at the bottom of the trench. As the least bit of root will grow it is not important to have a growth crown on every piece.

Plant in early spring and restrict above-ground growth to a main stem by removing side shoots. With good moist growing conditions, lifting should then start in the second season. I use my Dutch hoe to keep our horseradish bed free of weeds and also free of secondary horseradish growth to check the plant's invasive habit.

tender stems. I grow Earliest Purple which seems to have a slightly better flavour than the all-white variety Earliest White.

Sow: April–June
Distance between plants: 38 cm (15 in)
Distance between rows: 45 cm (18 in)
Harvest: July–October

VARIETIES:
Earliest White, sow April–May, matures in about 10 weeks, cook when still young and tender (smaller than a tennis ball).
Earliest Purple, more popular than its white counterpart, slightly more delicate flavour, my choice.

LEEKS. One of the hardiest winter vegetables – no matter how severe the frosts, they will survive unharmed.

The deeper the winter digging the better for leeks. In common with the rest of the onion family they appreciate a well-prepared soil containing plenty of well-rotted compost or manure plus an application of general fertiliser worked well in before planting. An occasional topdressing of fertiliser during the growing season is also beneficial.

Leeks do not do well in shade. I sow outside in a shallow drill in late March. The seedbed is brought to a fine tilth, and seed sown thinly so that seedlings are not crowded – crowding produces weak plants and can be a cause of bolting to seed later on.

Musselburgh and Lyon Prizetaker have done consistently well at Clack's Farm. By June the seedlings are about 15 cm (6 in) high and strong enough for transplanting. Plant with a dibber making 13-cm (5-in) deep holes 15 cm (6 in) apart in the row and then

drop a seedling into each hole. With a finger over the spout of the watering can, a dribble of water down the side of the hole washes in sufficient soil to cover the roots. Allow 30–38 cm (12–15 in) between rows.

As leeks grow I draw soil up around the stems to start the blanching process. The longer the length of blanched stem the better. Planting in a trench makes higher earthing up possible but takes more space.

Leeks for exhibition. For very early or exhibition leeks grow in a greenhouse in February. Prick out into small pots for hardening off in a cold frame before planting out in May. After germination these seedlings should be grown cool, standing them as near the glass as possible.

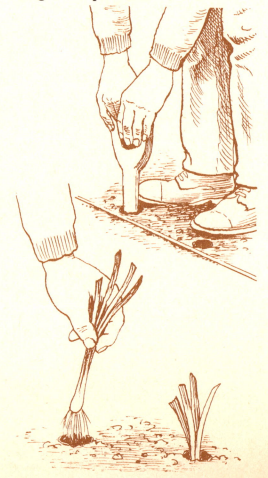

Making the planting holes for leeks

Watering the young plants

The exhibitor often pots on into 15-cm (6-in) pots to avoid a check – these early-sown leeks are so very liable to bolt. Show leeks are blanched in plastic sleeves, drain-pipes etc. Smaller leeks do not win prizes but they do keep well – even as late as April.

Sow: March
Plant: June
Planting depth: 13 cm (5 in)
Distance between plants: 15 cm (6 in)
Distance between rows: 30–38 cm (12–15 in)
Harvest: October–March

VARIETIES:
Lyon Prizetaker, a reliable variety, capable of making a great size when well grown.
Giant Winter, a variety to stay put in good condition for a long time.
Musselburgh, an old favourite, with excellent table qualities, more winter hardy than most other varieties.

LETTUCE. There is no lettuce to better the home grown and freshly cut. With a small greenhouse or garden frame its luxury can be enjoyed for at least eight months of the year.

For outdoor lettuce the ground should be well cultivated and have a good moisture-holding capacity. Well-rotted compost or manure will provide the moisture-holding sponge but neither should be applied when the ground is being prepared for the lettuce – the correct application time is 12 months previously. This allows excessive richness to be taken out by a previous crop and leaves the available level just right. Choose an open site. Shade produces weak growth and poor hearts.

My first outdoor lettuces come from a sowing of Fortune in my greenhouse in February. Although one of the butterhead type with a soft leaf it is good for early work. Sow thinly in a pan with the seed only just covered with a sprinkling of peat seed compost.

In a temperature of 13°C (55°F) germination takes only a few days. At temperatures above 16°C (60°F) lettuce seed germination is poor – above 18°C (65°F) it is almost nil.

As soon as the seedlings can be handled I prick them out into small peat pots. After a while they are hardened off in a cold frame ready for planting out under cloches towards the end of March. Under plastic cloches I manage to get two rows with 18 cm (9 in) between plants each way. It is best to allow 1 cm (½ in) between cloches for ventilation – an advantage not possible under plastic tunnels. Ventilation reduces the risk of disease.

As summer lettuces grow and mature more quickly than many other vegetables short rows for succession are easily fitted in between other crops such as rows of peas or brassicas. Sow little and often to avoid waste and bolting to seed – this occurs most frequently in midsummer when the weather is hot and dry. Watering obviously helps to keep the plants in good condition for longer at that time.

Sowing without protection starts in March. The seedbed tilth should be fine, dry

Cropping Plan for Lettuce

	Jan	Feb	Mar	Apr	May	Jun	Jul	Aug	Sep	Oct	Nov	Dec
Fortune		S	S	H	H	H						
Tom Thumb			S	S	H	H						
Avondefiance						S	S	S	H	H		
Continuity				S	S	H	H					
Suzan			S	S	S	H S	H S	H				
Windermere			S	S	S	H S	H S	H	H			
Webb's Wonderful					S	S	H	H				
Arctic King			H	H				S	S	S		
Imperial Winter			H	H	H				S			
Valdor				H	H				S			
Lobjoit's Green Cos		S	S			H	H					
Little Gem			S	S	S	H S	H S	H	H			
Paris White			S	S	S	H	H	H				
Winter Density			H	H	H		S		H	H S	H	
Kloek			H							S		
Kwiek								S			H	H
May Queen	S	S	H S	H	H	H				S	S	S

S = Sow   H = Harvest

on top and moist underneath. Sow thinly for thinning out to 18 cm (9 in) apart.

Again I sow Fortune followed by Suzan, rather pale leaved but a good butterhead type. Then I have Continuity, a favourite here – it is a smallish cabbage lettuce with bronze-tipped leaves and a tight, crisp heart. When the soil warms up in May I turn to the large, well-tried Webb's Wonderful which on our ground needs a full 30 cm (12 in) spacing after thinning.

Cos lettuces like warmer soil provided it is also moist. Small tight Little Gem is a space saver – 15 cm (6 in) spacing is sufficient. If I had to recommend just one summer lettuce it would be Little Gem. Its ability to stand unmoved by summer heat for weeks on end is almost enough commendation without reference to its superb quality. It is an ideal lettuce for small gardens.

I find the commercial growers' large cos Lobjoit's Green disappointing – with quantity of heart but not quality. For a large cos I choose Paris White. I find it hard to beat Winter Density (cos) sown in July for late autumn cutting. I sow it again in October to stand the winter, cloching part of the row after Christmas for cutting in March or April if the season is mild.

To keep the cold frame in use through the winter I sow and plant Arctic King. As under cloches, ventilation is needed to prevent losses from botrytis.

In an unheated greenhouse a short day variety such as Kwiek will produce leafy lettuce in November and December. Those fortunate enough to have a greenhouse and a little heat will find that Kloek sown in mid-October gives well-hearted lettuce in March. Choice of variety for winter growing is very important – only the short-day varieties will succeed.

When selecting lettuce to cut, check the condition of the heart by a little push with the back of the hand. Do not pinch – bruising starts rotting. Sparrows often peck at lettuce seedlings leaving them with too little leaf for survival. Cloches or tunnels are the complete answer – cottoning or plastic netting supported well above the plants is also effective.

Avondefiance, with its built-in resistance to mildew, has much to commend it for late summer and autumn cropping. Botrytis thrives in damp cold conditions, starting under the leaves and gradually rotting both leaf and stem. Air movement and warmth make attacks less likely.

Start with a moist, but not wet, planting bed and water carefully after planting – during the winter and in the early spring there should be sufficient moisture in the soil to carry the crop.

Aphids in various forms attack lettuce – spray with malathion. Where there are poplars nearby root aphids can be a problem. The aphids overwinter on poplar roots and move to lettuce roots in summer. Unless it is controlled, a massive root-aphid colony builds up and plant deaths follow. Water the plants with malathion at the first sign of root aphids.

Sow: August to March under glass
      March–September outside
Plant: March
Distance between plants: 15–30 cm (6–12 in)
Distance between rows: 30 cm (12 in)
Harvest: All the year round according to
      to variety

VARIETIES:
Cabbage Type (*summer*)
Fortune, a great lettuce, sown in the greenhouse and transplanted outside or sown outdoors from March onwards for succession.
Tom Thumb, the smallest lettuce grown, excellent quality, do not sow after the end of April.
Avondefiance, a variety bred for resistance to mildew, recommended for June to August sowings.
Continuity, a quality lettuce of medium size, outer leaves bronze tinted.
Suzan, can be sown from March to July for succession. A pale-hearted lettuce.
Windermere, a large crisp lettuce, sow for succession March to July.

Webb's Wonderful, still a good lettuce, large with a crisp heart, the original stock no longer available.

Cabbage Type (winter)
Arctic King, sow late August to October outdoors for cropping early spring. Extremely hardy, compact lettuce, not suitable for spring sowing.
Imperial Winter, hardy, larger than Arctic King, not suitable for spring sowing.
Valdor, a recent introduction for September sowing outdoors, makes a large lettuce in early spring, not suitable for spring sowing.

Cos Type
Lobjoit's Green Cos, a large lettuce, easy to grow for succession in the spring, lacks quality.
Little Gem, a truly great garden lettuce, crisp, full of flavour. Sow outdoors mid-March to July.
Paris White, very crisp and full of flavour.
Winter Density, a lettuce of excellent quality, crisp, suitable for both spring and autumn sowing, does well under cloches.

For Greenhouse or Cold Frame (winter)
Kloek, a well-hearted lettuce for cutting in early spring.
Kwiek, sown late August, will mature without heat from November to December.
May Queen, can be sown from October to March for cutting March to June, more resistant to botrytis than most varieties when grown without heat.

MARROWS. I sow marrow seeds on edge singly in 8-cm (3-in) pots using a peat seed compost and covering about 2·5 cm (1 in) deep. Sown in a greenhouse in mid-April

with a starting temperature of 16°C (60°F) germination takes place in a few days.

The plants are well spaced on the bench and later hardened off in a garden frame before planting out at the end of May or early June – it could be a fortnight earlier under cloches. Marrows are very easily damaged by frost.

There is no better growing medium than well-rotted compost. When I had an old-fashioned compost heap I always planted marrows on top. They enjoyed the diet, and during the season their roots rummaged about in the heap helping considerably with the breakdown process. Now with tidy compost bins operating I grow the marrows on the flat in saucer-like, water-conserving depressions but underneath each marrow goes a goodly quantity of well-rotted compost.

Long White will provide medium-sized marrows for ordinary use and winter storage. Marrows need plenty of watering in a dry season. To keep the plants cropping I occasionally add a liquid fertiliser to the water from July onwards.

Sow one marrow seed on edge in each pot, to avoid root disturbance when transplanting

Courgettes. I have stopped growing the trailing varieties as they take too much room. The newer, non-wandering, bush-type varieties suit me better. This year I am growing Zucchini, the original green courgette, and Golden Zucchini. The fruits of both I shall harvest and use when they are 10–15 cm (4–6 in) long.

Pumpkins. I do not understand why the pumpkin, so popular a member of the marrow family in America, is a joke here. The usual aim is to grow the largest in the district, and at this size there can only be complaints of lack of flavour. Small young pumpkins are to my mind better than marrows – the flesh is firmer. Sowing and growing is as for ordinary marrows.

If swelling pumpkins are cut young the cropping is continuous but if any are allowed to grow on to an enormous size, female flower and subsequent pumpkin production are slowed down. I grow Hundredweight or Mammoth – both will try hard to achieve their descriptive names.

Sow: April under glass
      May outside
Plant: May–June
Harvest: July–October

VARIETIES:
Marrow
Green Bush (F₁ hybrid), makes a compact plant, very free cropper especially when the marrows are cut small and regularly.
Tender and True, my favourite marrow, a medium-sized round marrow of real quality.
Long Green, a trailing variety which needs space to roam, can produce large marrows.
Long White, another trailing variety, the marrows store well.

Courgette
Golden Zucchini, a prolific cropper, the young marrows cooked as courgettes are delicious.
Zucchini, dark green fruits maturing early.

Pumpkin
Hundredweight, sow in the greenhouse end of April or outside end of May.
Mammoth, a large yellow pumpkin.

MINT. In one of its forms this is a must for the herb border. The foliage can be dried in summer for winter use.

Propagation is by burying portions of young, newly-lifted roots 5 cm (2 in) deep in spring. The difficulty of containing the growth is soon apparent. I hoe up to and around the clump, maintaining a chopped up 'no grow' area for the safety of the other herbs. Other methods of control such as planting in containers or plastic sheeting may be tried to avoid the vigilance required otherwise.

Each winter I lift and box a few roots to bring on in the greenhouse for early spring use. Apple mint is our favourite.

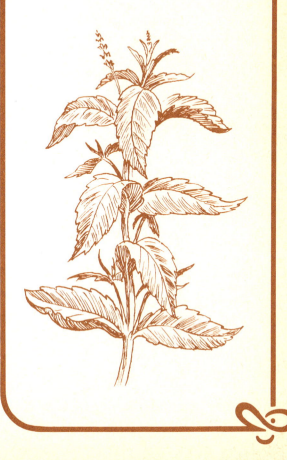

MUSTARD AND CRESS. For early season cutting sow in the greenhouse. Cress takes longer than mustard to reach the usable stage. After filling a shallow seed tray with seed compost sprinkle the cress seed on the surface – do not cover it. Water with a fine rose. Four days later sow the mustard in the same way. Both should be ready for cutting in about three weeks.

During spring and summer the technique can be employed outside.

Sow: All the year round
Harvest: 3 weeks after sowing

VARIETIES:
Mustard
White, sow 4 days after Curled Cress to come in at the same time for salad use.

Cress
Curled Cress, the real cress, sown either early in the greenhouse or later outside. For mustard and cress sow the cress seed 3 or 4 days ahead of the mustard.

ONIONS. No outdoor crop is more responsive to good treatment. A good onion reflects the skill of the gardener, as it is very demanding. Subject to freedom from white rot disease I grow onions on the same spot year after year and start preparing for the next season when the crop is cleared in September.

First comes autumn digging and incorporation of a liberal amount of well-rotted compost. I leave the top rough to gain maximum benefit from frost penetration. When the drying winds of March come I break the top down following an overall application of a Growmore type fertiliser at 100–140 g per sq m (3–4 oz per sq yd) completing stage one.

Onions will not tolerate weed competition without loss of crop so it is important to eliminate every scrap of perennial weed root.

The advantage of staying on one spot is twofold – the fertility level builds up gradually and as a result of intensive weeding over the years the weed problem decreases.

Sowing. Although I grow for the kitchen I still enjoy a crop of large onions turning the scale at 1·4 kg (3 lb) apiece. This means an early start – sowing in a propagating frame, with bottom heat and air temperature at 16°C (60°F), sometime between the end of December and the end of January.

I sow on the shortest day very thinly in a peat seed compost, only lightly covering the seed and watering with a fine rose immediately afterwards. Germination takes about a fortnight.

I prick out the strongest seedlings while they are still in the loop stage, putting them singly into peat pots containing a peat potting compost. From then onwards they are grown cool and finally hardened off in a cold frame. If at any time temperatures are too high, the plants become weak, and despite apparent recovery this means a reduction in the harvested weight.

While the seedlings should never be allowed to go short of water, overwatering brings the risk of damping off. Should this happen, spray or water the seedlings with benomyl diluted according to the directions on the pack.

Plant out in mid-April. I plant 20 cm (8 in) apart – for exhibition onions 25 cm (10 in) would be better. Do not plant too deeply – only the roots should be in the ground, not the stem. Allow 30 cm (1 ft) between rows.

Keep the bed clean throughout the season. Give an occasional application of general fertiliser between the rows. I grow Ailsa Craig and Mammoth Improved.

Direct sowing. Direct-sown onions sown in March or April in rows 30 cm (1 ft) apart for harvesting at the end of August are never as large as those grown from transplants, but they keep much longer. If onions are to keep, the variety must be right and they must be planted firmly, well harvested and stored with good ventilation.

In my experience Bedfordshire Champion, Improved Reading and Rijnsburger Yellow Globe are among the best. The seedbed must be firm with a fine top tilth. Before sowing I dress my onion seed with a white fungicidal seed dressing which makes even distribution of hitherto black seed along the drill easier. Before covering I sprinkle bromophos granules along the drill as a first precaution against onion fly.

Do not sow deeper than 1 cm (½ in) – I just lightly cover, then firm the length of the row with the head of the rake. Never pull green onions from the main onion bed. The risk of onion fly is so much greater after disturbance.

Apart from taking onion fly precautions, grow direct-sown onions as transplanted onions. I never wait for onion fly to strike. As soon as the seedlings straighten out of the loop stage I water along the rows with a dilute solution of gamma HCH.

Sets. Specially-prepared onion sets make growing easier because the risk of onion fly is almost nil. When purchased the sets should be dormant without a trace of leaf growth. Keep them like this until planting time – March or early April – by opening the package and storing in a light, cool, but frost-free place.

I plant sets 23 cm (9 in) apart in the row using a trowel to make the small planting hole. The tip of the set should just show above ground after firming around gently with the fingers. Do not push the sets into the ground as this firms the soil underneath and in time they are pushed out again by their own roots.

I grow Stuttgarter Giant which produces large flat onions that keep well beyond Christmas. I am also trying Coronado, which is a high quality round onion capable of keeping until late spring.

The ripening, harvesting and storing of onions demands care. When the tops show signs of dying down, easing up each bulb

Plant onion set firmly 23 cm (9 in) apart

slightly with a hand fork speeds up the process. Do not leave ripe onions too long in the row undisturbed – as colder, damper conditions approach, botrytis (grey mould) is liable to set in and ruin what would have been a good crop. I lay the almost ripe onions on their sides exposing the base to the sun.

On a dry day when ripening is complete I gather the onions for stringing up or laying out on a bench. After that, satisfactory storage depends on good ventilation and cool, light conditions.

Sow: December–January under glass
     March–April outside
Plant: April
Plant sets: March–April
Distance between plants: 20–25 cm (8–10 in)
Distance between rows: 30 cm (12 in)
Harvest: August–September

VARIETIES:
Raising from Seed:
Ailsa Craig, a large white onion, suitable for January sowing in the greenhouse for transplanting outside in the spring or for direct sowing outside in March.
Bedfordshire Champion, a well-tried variety for sowing outside in March, excellent keeper when well harvested.
Blood Red, a very firm dark red onion of medium size, excellent keeper.
Improved Mammoth, a really large onion, much favoured by the exhibitor, has been grown and shown weighing more than 2·25 kg (5 lb) each. Sow in the greenhouse between the end of December and the end of January for transplanting outside in the spring.
Improved Reading, a flat-shaped onion for sowing outside in March, one of the best keepers.
Mammoth Red, the largest red onion grown, an onion for the exhibitor and ordinary gardener, a good keeper. Sow as for Improved Mammoth.
Paris Silverskin, very quick-growing quality onion for pickling, sow fairly thickly March to June.
Rijnsburger Yellow Globe, a yellow-skinned white-fleshed variety, with good-keeping qualities.
Sturon, a quality round onion for direct sowing outside in March, a good keeper.

Raising from Sets:
Coronado, a recent introduction from Denmark, makes a large round onion, straw-coloured skin, mild flavour, very good keeper.
Stuttgarter Giant, very popular flat onion, mild flavour, keeps well.

Japanese Onions

The seed of several varieties of Japanese onions has been introduced, and they are sown in August for harvesting the following June. The August sowing dates are critical and determined by geographical location. Here in Worcestershire I sow in the second week of August – as other direct-onion sowings. The plants stand the winter unharmed by frost.

Do not use this seed for spring sowing, nor try to transplant, although thinning out in spring is advisable. Of the two varieties I have tried I prefer the quality and mild flavour of Express Yellow to Kaizuka Extra Early.

Sow: August
Distance between plants: 20 cm (8 in)
Distance between rows: 30 cm (12 in)
Harvest: June

VARIETIES:
Express Yellow, a Japanese flat onion, sow at the end of August for picking the next June, a very good keeper.
Kaizuka Extra Early, strong growing Japanese onion which ripens to a pale yellow colour.

Shallots

A hardy perennial form of onion is the shallot, which when planted as a single bulb multiplies six or eight fold during the growing season. I still find shallots the best onions for pickling. I grow Giant Yellow and Long Keeping Yellow.

The secret of success is to give the crop a long-growing season – the sooner the bulbs are planted after the shortest day the better. In summer, ripening starts after the longest day with the leaves slowly turning yellow. When the leaves are completely yellow, harvest the bulbs and dry in the sun.

Plant: January–February
Distance between plants: 15 cm (6 in)
Distance between rows: 30 cm (12 in)
Harvest: June–July

VARIETIES:
Giant Yellow, planted early in the New Year for harvesting and pickling in June.
Long Keeping Yellow, a variety with a reputation for keeping well in store.

Spring Onions

For spring onions I sow a row of White Lisbon in March and repeat as required until August. In September, for the earliest spring onions I sow White Lisbon-Winter Hardy which as its name implies, can withstand heavy frost.

Sow: March–September
Distance between rows: 30 cm (12 in)
Harvest: March–October

VARIETIES:
White Lisbon, sow March to August for pulling green, mild flavour.
White Lisbon–Winter Hardy, sow in September to stand the winter, for pulling green in the spring, not suitable for spring sowing.

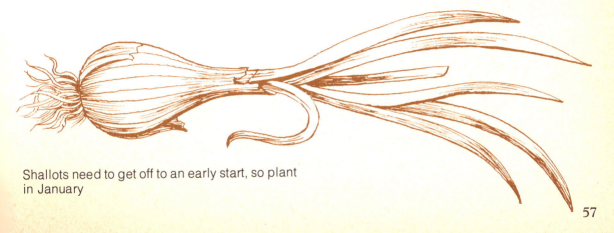

Shallots need to get off to an early start, so plant in January

P

PARSLEY. This is grown from seed and thinned to, or planted out at, 23 cm (9 in) apart. Outside the problem can be finding the seedlings among the weeds. Parsley seed can take up to five weeks to germinate, which puts the weed seedlings ahead. For this reason I sow indoors (a windowsill would do) and prick out into small peat pots for planting outside.

To ensure a continuous supply of green parsley I sow in March and again in July. The later batch takes over when the first has run to seed. Carrot fly can kill parsley immediately after planting out so I water with a solution of gamma HCH. The same treatment may be given to plants grown directly from seed. I choose a curled variety such as Curly Top or Perfection. Cloche protection in winter keeps the foliage good.

VARIETIES:
Curly Top, compact grower, dark green, slow to run to seed.
Imperial Curled, closely curled leaves, dark green, compact, slow to run to seed, of excellent flavour.
Perfection, compact grower, dark green very finely curled.
Hamburg Parsley, grown for its parsnip-like root, which is cooked as a vegetable, the foliage is used for soup flavouring.

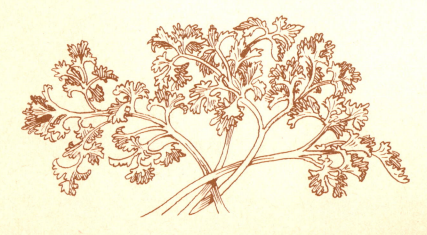

PARSNIPS. An easily-grown root vegetable for winter use with no storage problems. They keep well in the ground provided it does not flood – in fact after frost the flavour is improved.

Most varieties are long-rooted so the easier the going the better are the chances of long straight parsnips. Double digging used to be a standard preparatory practice, or else 60-cm (2-ft) deep holes were made with a crowbar and filled with a soil mixture that would offer no resistance. The latter is an exhibitor's method.

On no account should fresh manure or rich compost be worked in immediately prior to parsnip growing but the earlier the digging is done the better. Sowing can start in February if the weather is favourable – sow in March at the latest.

Old seed may deteriorate unless kept in an air-tight packet. I sow fresh seed in shallow drills, putting three or four seeds at each position 23 cm (9 in) apart – this will make singling easier.

I grow Tender and True and Hollow Crown. On a shallow soil a shorter-rooted variety such as Intermediate or White Gem would be better. Parsnip canker (soft brown areas on the shoulder) is a trouble on some soils in which case the choice should be Avonresister – bred especially for its resistance to canker.

Sow: February–March
Distance between plants: 23 cm (9 in)
Distance between rows: 45 cm (1½ ft)
Harvest: November–March

VARIETIES:
Avonresister, a variety bred to resist parsnip canker, a disease which attacks the shoulder of the parsnip.
Hollow Crown, a well-proven variety, long white root, excellent flavour.
Tender and True, my first choice, excellent quality, fairly resistant to parsnip canker.
White Gem, a short parsnip, especially suitable for growing on shallow soils, a good quality root of excellent flavour.

Growing parsnips by the crowbar method

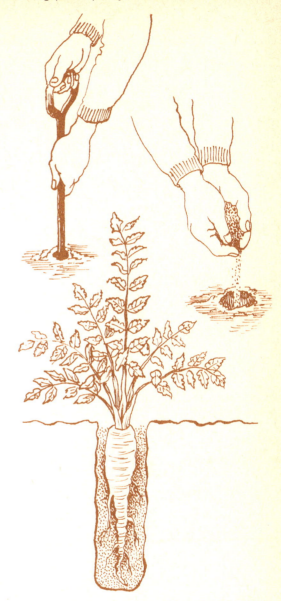

PEAS. When I was a boy we grew the tall variety Alderman which needed 2-m (6-ft) pea sticks. Since then dwarf-growing varieties have been developed with heights from 30 cm–1 m (1–3 ft). I give them some support to keep the pods off the ground – twigs, or just a few short canes with a couple of strings both sides of the row.

I prepare the ground well, including some well-rotted compost and making an overall application of general fertiliser before the final seedbed preparation. This is followed by a light dressing of hydrated lime along the proposed length of the row. Peas object to an acid soil.

For the earliest crop on well-drained soil, sow a round-seeded variety such as Feltham First in late October or November. Seed dressed with a fungicide germinates successfully and the plants stand the winter.

Round-seeded peas should be used for the first early sowings in the New Year – they do not have the table qualities of the wrinkled-seeded ones but the latter must not be sown before mid-March.

Cloches bring picking dates forward by about a month. Under cloches I sow radish one side of the pea row and the lettuce Fortune the other. A 'V'-shaped drill 5 cm (2 in) deep can be used for sowing but I prefer to make a spade-wide, 5-cm (2-in)-deep trench and space the peas 5 cm (2 in) apart in three rows along the flat base.

After covering the seed I settle the top with a rake head. I then set a mousetrap under a box with two mouse-sized entry holes. (A brick goes on the box to weight it against the inquisitiveness of other animals.) A single mouse can ruin a row of peas.

The run of supports should be fixed just after germination – once the plants are on the floor it is hard to get them up satisfactorily.

I choose a succession of varieties rather than repeats of one variety. In March I start sowing wrinkled varieties carrying on in the following order: Little Marvel – 50 cm (20 in), Early Onward – 60 cm (2 ft), Kelvedon Wonder – 45 cm (18 in), Onward – 60 cm (2 ft), and for summer cropping Senator – 1 m (3 ft), in my opinion the best flavoured of the dwarf peas.

For an autumn crop I sow Kelvedon Wonder at the beginning of July. Of the dwarf, wrinkled varieties it is the least susceptible to mildew – a problem particularly associated with an autumn crop. I have tried varieties such as Gullivert, Purple Podded and Sugar Dwarf but with space at a premium I regard them as of academic interest only.

Pests include pea moth – responsible for maggots inside the pod. Spray with a solution of gamma HCH in the evening about a week after flowering starts, and repeat 10 days later. Pea weevil may nibble at the leaf edges – again gamma HCH is the answer.

Sow: February–July, October–November
Distance between plants: 5 cm (2 in)
Distance between rows: 60 cm–1·25 m (2 ft–4 ft)
Harvest: May–October

VARIETIES:
Early
Early Onward, a wrinkled pea, sow March onwards, heavy cropper, excellent quality, freezes well. Height 60 cm (2 ft).
Feltham First, a round-seeded pea, suitable for very early sowing, does well under cloches, only fair quality. Height 45 cm (1½ ft).
Kelvedon Wonder, a wrinkled pea, sow March onwards, one of the best for sowing late July on account of its great resistance to mildew. Excellent quality. Height 45 cm (1½ ft).
Little Marvel, a wrinkled pea, an old favourite, sow March onwards, well suited for growing under cloches, excellent quality. Height 50 cm (20 in).
Pilot, a round-seeded pea for early sowing, heavy cropper, fair quality. Height 1·15 m (3½ ft).

Second Early
Hurst Green Shaft, a wrinkled pea, sow March onwards, heavy cropper, pods produced in pairs, resistant to mildew, good quality. Height 60 cm (2 ft).
Onward, a wrinkled pea, sow March onwards, very popular, heavy cropper, excellent quality, one of the best for freezing. Height 60 cm (2 ft).
Senator, a maincrop variety, sow in March onwards, light-coloured pods filled with peas of great quality. Height 1 m (3 ft).
Show Perfection, a wrinkled pea, a variety for the exhibitor, excellent quality, freezes well. Height 1·25–1·5 m (4–5 ft).

PEPPERS (CAPSICUM). These do well in hot summers in the South, outside as well as in unheated greenhouses. As with other tender plants, success outside depends on the season.

My growing has been in an unheated house from seed (New Ace) sown in a propagating frame in March: 16–18°C (60–65°F) gives good germination. The seedlings are pricked out singly into 8-cm (3-in) pots, then in May either potted on into 20-cm (8-in) pots or planted three to a peat growing bag. In the absence of a growing check the plants will become bushy naturally. A check such as pot-binding produces a single stem that will need to have the main growing tip pinched out.

I give a high potash liquid fertiliser at a third of the rate recommended for tomatoes. Watch for plant lice (a form of aphid) on the undersides of the leaves, and spray with malathion when seen.

Choose the sunniest position for outdoor planting and wait until June when there is no longer any frost risk. Cloche protection is an advantage. Unripe fruits are green peppers – left to ripen they become red peppers.

Sow: March under glass
Plant: June
Harvest: July–September

VARIETIES:

New Ace (F₁ hybrid), a variety I have grown since its introduction, it crops early and is very well suited for growing in a small greenhouse.
Outdoor, a variety recommended for growing under cloches in the warmer districts.
Worldbeater, a reliable variety for the greenhouse, also suitable for outdoors in the South, either under cloches or in a sheltered position.

POTATOES. The best crop for cleaning newly-broken ground. I have never known them to be overcome by weed competition if the necessary cultivation has been done well.

Until recently I recommended gardeners to concentrate on early potatoes leaving the maincrop to farmers, but increased shop prices have intervened.

Potatoes do best on medium soils. On very light soils the addition of organic manures, and watering in exceptionally dry periods, is essential. Wet, heavy soils, even well worked, may involve slug damage and autumn harvesting problems.

Once a plot is clean, fit potatoes into a crop rotation plan ensuring that they are only grown on any one section once in three years. Breaking this rule can lead to the establishment of potato eelworm.

As an extra safeguard, wash your seed potatoes in clean water before setting them up in trays and maintain the humus level in the soil. Humus supports fungi that prey on the eelworm – hence the need for routine digging in of organic matter (compost).

Planting. Plant on an open site – in shade potato tops are drawn and cropping is seldom good. The ideal size for a seed potato is that of a hen's egg. Cutting tubers lengthways into two or more pieces is worth doing – each piece must have sprouts. Dust the cut surface with hydrated lime and plant immediately.

In addition to compost I apply a Growmore-type fertiliser along the open trench before planting. Lawn mowings or peat around the tubers bring an improvement where disfiguring potato scab is a problem.

I plant first early varieties in rows 68 cm (2 ft 3 in) apart with 30 cm (12 in) between tubers – second earlies and maincrop varieties with 75 cm (2 ft 6 in) between rows and 38 cm (15 in) between tubers.

On freshly-broken ground it is easiest to plant with a spade digging a 13-cm (5-in) deep hole for each tuber. On well-cultivated ground open up a trench 15 cm (6 in) deep, put some well-rotted compost in the bottom and plant on that. Use a garden line as the rows need to be straight for future cultivations.

The usual planting time is March or April. Once the first growth appears frost can do

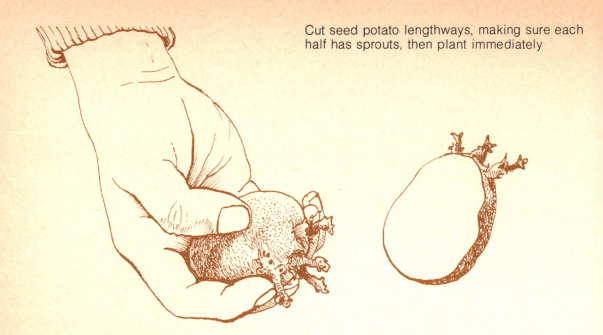

Cut seed potato lengthways, making sure each half has sprouts, then plant immediately

Storing maincrop potatoes in a clamp after they have dried off. Pile tubers on a layer of straw, cover with more straw 15 cm (6 in) deep. Finally cover with a 23 cm (9 in) layer of beaten earth pierced by a wisp of straw at the top for ventilation

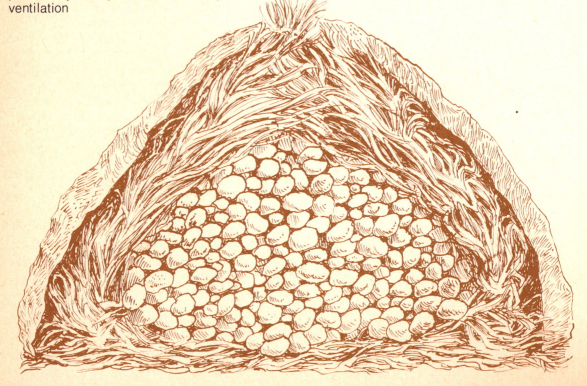

damage, so for as long as practicable I draw soil over the tops when frost is forecast. When the tops are bigger, newspapers will suffice. If the worst does happen new growth will come again – the only loss being time.

Sprouted tubers give the best start. Set up the seed to sprout in a tray, with eyes upward, in a light, cool but frost-free place.

First earlies planted in March are usually ready for lifting in July, but by using cloches to warm the ground before planting and for covering the planted rows until the haulms outgrow them, I can enjoy new potatoes in June.

Extending the season. Aiming at a longer new potato season I plant Foremost singly in 25-cm (10-in) pots (peat potting compost) in February in my greenhouse. Kept near the light and fed with a liquid fertiliser, the plants crop for Easter.

For Christmas I plant sprouted seed of first early varieties in July, having kept a tray of seed back specially. The seed is stored outside during June so the sprouts are strong and short. Autumn frosts may cut down the haulms but in our light, medium soil the potatoes keep well, and new, into December. On heavy, slug-plagued soil it would be necessary to lift after the first frost and store in damp peat or suchlike away from the light.

Harvesting and storing. Pick a dry day for harvesting maincrop potatoes, so that after lifting they can stay on top a few hours to dry off. I store in a straw and earth-covered clamp with a wisp of straw in the top as a ventilator. Storage in a box or hessian sack in a dark shed is all right, but do not use polythene bags.

Potato blight is not usually a problem in industrial areas – the choice of less susceptible varieties reduces the risk in rural areas. If blight does appear in September cut off and remove the haulms to prevent spores being washed down to the tubers.

Aphids spread virus diseases from plant to plant leading to a reduction in cropping capacity. Complete control is almost impossible in some districts – hence the specialised seed potato production in Scotland and Ireland.

The Ministry of Agriculture inspects potato crops intended for seed and in appropriate cases issues certificates of health. Look for the certificate at the time of purchase. Saving one's own seed may be all right for one season but I do not advise going on longer. My first early variety is Foremost, followed by Duke of York, Epicure and Desirée.

Earlies:
Plant: March
Distance between tubers: 30 cm (12 in)
Distance between rows: 68 cm (2 ft 3 in)
Harvest: June–July

VARIETIES:
Duke of York, kidney shaped, cream-fleshed potato, very good flavour.
Epicure, very early cropper, round with rather deep eyes, renowned for its flavour.
Foremost, very early, heavy cropper of round tubers, good flavour, inclined to be wet.
Sharpe's Express, kidney shaped, white-fleshed potato, fair cropper, excellent flavour.

Maincrop:
Plant: March–April
Distance between tubers: 38 cm (15 in)
Distance between rows: 75 cm (2½ ft)
Harvest: September

VARIETIES:
Desirée, a recently introduced variety, red-skinned cream-fleshed tubers, heavy cropper, good flavour.
Golden Wonder, the finest flavoured late potato, cream fleshed, light cropper except on high fertility land.
Kerr's Pink, the most popular late potato in Scotland, great quality, floury when cooked.
Majestic, an old favourite, still crops well, white potato much favoured for chipping.
Pink Fir Apple, the potato *par excellence* for a potato salad. Tubers rather sausage shaped, makes copious haulm growth.

PUMPKIN, see Marrow.

RADISH. Not only the easiest salad crop to grow, but also very quick. When the soil warms up in the spring, tender radishes are ready to eat four weeks after sowing.

This makes radish the catch crop for sowing alongside a row of cloched peas early in the season, or between slower-maturing crops or on the ridges of a celery trench. Earlier radishes can be sown in a greenhouse.

All soils other than heavy wet clays are suitable. Radishes will grow in light shade, but under these conditions tend to make more leaf.

Sow thinly in rows or else broadcast and rake in the seed lightly. If the soil is very dry, water with a fine rose after sowing. Overcrowding produces tops rather than roots. Always pull young – if radishes are left too long they get pithy and hot.

I always grow French Breakfast and Cherry Belle, and a few others such as White Icicle. A packet of mixed seed is worth a try.

Winter radish. As well as summer radishes, hardy winter varieties such as China Rose and Black Spanish can be grown for winter cropping. In severe weather it is wise to give them a covering of straw or similar material. Winter radishes are very large – sometimes 340 g (¾ lb) or more – so they are usually shredded or sliced for salad.

Sow: October–February under glass
March–September outside
Harvest: February–November

VARIETIES:
Cherry Belle, my favourite, sow for succession March to September, bright-red, round radish, mild flavour.
French Breakfast, an ever popular variety, half red and half white.
White Icicle, a crisp, white radish.

Winter Radishes
Black Spanish, large and round with white flesh and black skin.
China Rose, sow in August, leave in the ground until wanted for winter salads.

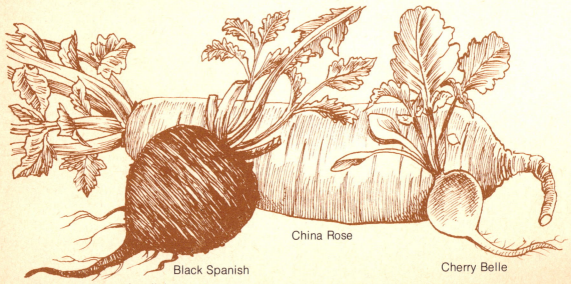

China Rose

Black Spanish

Cherry Belle

The different shapes of radishes

ROSEMARY. An attractive as well as a useful plant for the herb garden. The common green-leaf form is more hardy than the gold or silver-striped varieties.

Without the additional use of the foliage for making rosemary tea the plant is worth its place for the flavour it adds to meat dishes – particularly lamb.

I also enjoy the refreshing aroma of shoots gently pressed in the hand in passing.

Rosemary is easily propagated from 15-cm (6-in) cuttings taken in summer or from seed sown in spring. Give it an open position with protection in a severe winter. It will be especially happy on sandy soil.

SAGE is a herb for every vegetable garden – it is so easy to grow and manage and is useful in the kitchen either fresh or dried. The common green sage is evergreen although its foliage looks tired after severe frost.

Give sage a dry sunny spot. I start mine by taking cuttings with a heel during the summer. They root easily in a shady position ready for transplanting in early autumn. On our slightly acid soil I give the planting area a light dusting of lime before digging out the hole.

After two or three years the plants get straggly and I begin again with young rooted stock. The purple and variegated foliage forms are attractive in flower and leaf as well as being suitable for culinary use.

SEAKALE. This was a luxury vegetable in the past but is easy to grow and force despite the traditional forcing pots being no longer available.

Propagation is from pieces of side root about 13 cm (5 in) long. Cut the top end level and the other slanting – this identifies top and bottom – planting five pieces round the sides of a 13-cm (5-in) pot in early spring in a greenhouse.

The first growth will be a ring of tiny shoots. Remove carefully all but the strongest few, and finally, before planting, retain only the strongest single shoot, which will eventually make a crown for forcing.

In autumn I lift the crowns ready for forcing in the dark. Our cellar, with a constant temperature of 10°C (50°F), is ideal. Single crowns with shortened roots are planted in 20-cm (8-in) pots and kept moist to ensure growth – under our conditions forcing takes about six weeks. All the forced growth must be without colour or it will be bitter.

Crowns may be left in the ground and forced by covering with lightproof material, but then it is spring before the blanched seakale is ready.

Plant: March
Lift for forcing: October–November
Harvest: November–February

SEAKALE BEET (**Swiss Chard**). Here are two distinct vegetables for the table. The thick white leaf stems and ribs, striped of the leafy part, are delicious cooked like asparagus, and in contrast the green leaf is similar to spinach.

Propagate seakale by cutting the side roots into thongs

Before forcing reduce the shoots to leave the strongest one

Sow in 4-cm (1½-in) deep drills at the end of April or early May. Cropping will begin in July and go on throughout the summer. I space the seed two or three to a position 30 cm (12 in) apart in the drill, singling out to the strongest seedling later on.

Pre-sowing soil preparation can include the incorporation of well-rotted compost to help the soil moisture supply in dry weather. Watering in hot, dry spells does much to keep up the replacement of leaves.

Sow: April–May
Distance between plants: 30 cm (12 in)
Distance between rows: 45 cm (18 in)
Harvest: July–September

VARIETIES:
Seakale Beet (Swiss Chard), grown for it's leaf, the green tissue cooks like spinach and the white main ribs of the leaves are cooked separately (poor man's asparagus), does not produce an edible root.

SHALLOTS, see Onions

SPINACH. This is widely regarded as a health food – the green leaf being so full of iron and vitamins. Poor cooking techniques, resulting in sogginess, often make spinach undeservedly unpopular – it needs growing well and cooking well.

In its several forms, spinach can be grown as a catch or follow-on crop. Summer spinach sown in March or April produces more leaf when the early summer is cool and moist – in hot dry weather the plants tend to bolt to seed without making much usable leaf. Bolting is more likely on light soils, therefore add well-rotted compost to the soil at winter digging time.

To maintain a continuity of supply make successional sowings up to August. I sow Greenmarket and Sigmaleaf.

After sowing thinly in shallow drills I thin the seedlings to 23 cm (9 in) apart – 30 cm

(12 in) would be needed between rows. A September sowing of Greenmarket produces an excellent early spring crop of large leaf.

For cropping from November onwards try Long Standing Prickly. The leaf is different but it is good quality and winter hardy.

Sow: March–September
Distance between plants: 23 cm (9 in)
Distance between rows: 30 cm (12 in)
Harvest: May to March

VARIETIES:
Greenmarket, a high yielding variety which tolerates winter conditions.
Long Standing Round, sow for succession March–July, pick regularly.
Long Standing Prickly, quick growing, for picking in winter and spring.
Sigmaleaf, can be sown in spring, or autumn for over-wintering.
Viking, sow for succession March–July, dark green leaves, pick regularly.

New Zealand Spinach
New Zealand is for summer cropping. With its trailing habit it spreads, and produces thick fleshy leaves which it has a capacity to replace after each picking; this makes it a real 'cut-and-come-again' spinach during the summer months.

Sowing time is late April or May. As the seed is very hard, most seed firms suggest soaking it overnight prior to sowing. New Zealand spinach is a good alternative on hot dry soils where ordinary spinach always bolts. As the plants are frost sensitive avoid late sowings.

Sow: April–May
Distance between plants: 23 cm (9 in)
Distance between rows: 30 cm (12 in)
Harvest: June–September

SPINACH BEET (Perpetual Spinach). This is grown for its large-leaf foliage. When pulled regularly the foliage is continuously replaced by new growth. In a hot dry summer

that sends ordinary spinach to seed this type just goes on and on, providing both quality and quantity.

For the longest period of use make two sowings – first in March and again in July. The later sowing does well for autumn and winter pickings.

I sow in 4-cm (1½-in) deep drills, spacing groups of seeds in positions 30 cm (12 in) apart. Single out later to leave a strong seedling at each position. Take advantage of this beet's ability to withstand drought, but water it at such times to keep up the quality of the leaf.

Sow: March and July
Distance between plants: 30 cm (12 in)
Distance between rows: 30 cm (12 in)
Harvest: June–April

SWEDE.

As swede is a brassica it should be fitted into the area allocated to brassicas in the crop rotation plan, to minimise the risk of club root.

Swedes are hardier than turnips and milder in flavour. In the small, enclosed vegetable garden mildew can be a real problem, but by delaying sowing until May in the North, and late May in the South, the risk is reduced. Even so a preventive fungicide treatment (zineb or liquid copper) in late August is advisable.

In addition to my chosen varieties Purple Top and Acme (both of excellent quality), Chignecto, bred to resist club root, can be useful to those specially concerned about the disease.

Before sowing I give a light overall application of hydrated lime. I sow in drills 2 cm

Pick over spinach beet throughout the summer months to ensure a constant supply of foliage

(¾ in) deep and rows 45 cm (18 in) apart.

In very dry, hot weather flea beetles will attack the emerging seedlings. A dusting with derris powder along the row will put a stop to their tricks.

Thinning out the seedlings to a minimum 30 cm (12 in) apart reduces the chances of a mildew problem. I find that swedes keep better left in the ground in autumn than lifted and stored above ground, but I realise that I rely a great deal on my light, quick-draining soil as a storage medium.

Sow: May
Distance between plants: 30 cm (12 in)
Distance between rows: 45 cm (18 in)
Harvest: October–December

VARIETIES:
Acme, a swede of good flavour.
Bronze Top, smaller than Purple Top.
Purple Top, excellent winter vegetable.

SWEET CORN. Luxurious corn on the cob comes from a plant revelling in a warm season. Recent plant breeding successes, and the introduction of early maturing F_1 hybrids, have made it possible for those of us living in the southern half of the country at least to sow and plant outside every year with a good hope of success.

A greenhouse or even propagator on a windowsill, with the seed sown in April singly in small pots, gets the plants off to an early start. The outdoor planting site should be sunny, sheltered and well-prepared – but not too richly manured if excessively lush leaf growth is to be avoided.

As cob production depends on efficient pollination, both the high-up tassels of male flowers, and female flowers from which the cobs develop, are present on each plant. Nevertheless, within reason the nearer the plants are together the better. I grow a square block of plants 20 cm (8 in) apart each way – not only is pollination better but also the plants protect each other from wind damage.

Test sweet corn for ripeness by puncturing a grain with a finger nail

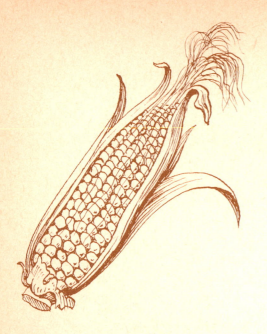

For the earliest cobs I grow First of All which is shorter than most, and to follow I have Kelvedon Glory. For freezing and fresh use the cobs should be gathered young before the grains harden and lose their flavour.

I check by slightly opening the covering sheath to expose a few grains. Punctured with a finger nail when nearly ready, a grain will exude a clear liquid – in a day or so this sap will be milky and the cob ripe for picking.

Sow: April under glass
Plant: May–June
Distance between plants: 18 cm (15 in)
each way
Harvest: July–September

VARIETIES:
First of All, my favourite, sown in the greenhouse late April, planted under cloches late May, ready in July/August, excellent quality.
Kelvedon Glory, later than First of All, large cobs, excellent quality.
North Star, a reliable variety for Northern districts, good quality.

SWISS CHARD. see Seakale Beet

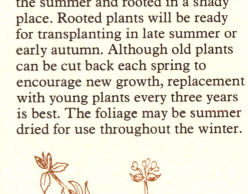

THYME. Common thyme or lemon thyme are best for general use. They produce small-leafed aromatic foliage in quantity and will tolerate frequent gathering. Plant in the open in well-drained, not-too-heavy soil.

Propagate simply from 8-cm (3-in) heeled cuttings taken during the summer and rooted in a shady place. Rooted plants will be ready for transplanting in late summer or early autumn. Although old plants can be cut back each spring to encourage new growth, replacement with young plants every three years is best. The foliage may be summer dried for use throughout the winter.

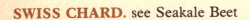

TOMATOES.

TOMATOES. In a greenhouse no other crop is capable of so much edible produce over so long a period. Growing one's own plants from seed in a heated greenhouse is a straightforward job.

Planting out from such a start can be done early and it is just a question of waiting a while in the New Year for the quality of light to improve, as light is as important as warmth. Without good light, growth is weak, fruit set is poor and crop yields low, so keep greenhouse glass clean and the framework down to a minimum.

Importance of variety. Choice of variety is all important. For me, home-grown tomatoes must turn out to be better than I can buy. The commercial grower considers cropping capacity, travelling ability, shelf-life and eye appeal but has no need to be around at the tasting stage.

I require flavour first – after that a reasonably thin skin. Also having a compact plant with its fruit trusses close-spaced on the mainstem is of special importance in a small greenhouse.

The variety must be free from greenback (a tough unripenable green shoulder on the fruit), not too subject to tomato leaf mould, and, finally, be a good cropper capable of early ripening.

In recent years I have grown Alicante, which meets all my requirements; Golden Queen, a good-flavoured, golden-fruited variety; Tangella, with excellent tangerine-coloured fruits but too spreading a habit for a small greenhouse, and Tigerella which has tiger-striped red fruits. There are many other good varieties but whatever you grow do make your choice on quality – if not the reward will be an ordinary crop when it could be extra special.

Cultivation in the greenhouse. Tomato plants need a day temperature of about 16°C (60°F) and a slightly lower night temperature. I can manage this from March onwards.

In early February I sow the seed at about 30 seeds to a 9-cm (3½-in) pot in a peat-based compost, covering it lightly before watering with a fine rose. In a propagating frame on a greenhouse bench in 16–18°C (60–65°F) the seed takes only a few days to germinate.

I prick the seedlings out singly into 8-cm (3-in) pots in peat potting compost as soon as the seed leaves straighten out. Experience has shown me that by so doing, the bottom trusses develop more flowers. From then on it is a question of careful watering, and good spacing on the bench to avoid crowding and weak growth.

Problems with soil. After erecting a new greenhouse on either virgin soil or soil which has not previously been used for growing tomatoes, it is safe to expect at least two or three years of tomato growing without running into trouble from pests or disease. From then on the risk is likely to increase until it is impossible to keep them alive long enough to start producing tomatoes. In addition to the probable build up of diseases, such as verticillium wilt (sleepy disease), or pests like tomato eelworm, the repeated application of fertilisers sometimes results in an excess of certain salts in the soil. This makes normal functioning of the plant metabolism unsatisfactory.

In years past it was common practice to completely change the border soil every two or three years. However this would only be successful if all the soil was dug out completely and replaced to a depth of at least 1 m (3 ft). An alternative was to sterilise the soil using steam or chemicals, neither of which were very practical propositions for the owners of a small greenhouse.

1. Dig out a trench in the greenhouse border 13 cm (5 in) deep

2. Fill with aggregate, making sure the surface is level

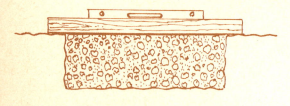

3. Place ring in position and fill with compost

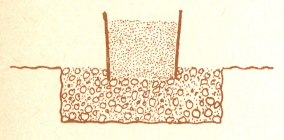

4. Plant young tomato in ring

Ring Culture. Ring culture overcomes the whole range of problems by encouraging the plants to develop a two-tier root system. The top tier of roots grow within a 25-cm (10-in) bottomless bituminised 'ring' or bottomless pot, of either plastic or clay. These bottomless rings stand on a 13-cm (5-in) deep base of either coarse ashes, pea-sized washed gravel or peat into which the bottom tier of roots develop soon after planting out. For ring culture the plants should not be potbound. With full root action the get away is so much quicker and the critical task of getting the roots to grow without delay is achieved.

It is often recommended to lay a sheet of plastic under the aggregate, however I have never regretted not doing so. With proper feeding and watering the roots should not stray outside the aggregate, where plastic sheeting would create waterlogging and, consequently, root damage.

I dig out the border soil to a depth of 13 cm (5 in), and infill with aggregate, making sure the surface of both the soil and the aggregate above it are level, otherwise even watering is impossible. When this is done the ring can be placed in position, being spaced so that each plant is 38 cm (15 in), or better still, 95 cm (18 in) from its neighbour. Fill each ring to within 5 cm (2 in) of the top with John Innes Compost No. 3. I try to get the rings filled a few days ahead of planting to allow time for the compost to warm up slightly (cold compost can give a young plant a severe growth check).

After planting, water each plant in thoroughly. This should suffice until rooting into the aggregate is well under way. From then on regular watering of the aggregate will encourage the roots to grow down in search of moisture. Do not water again through the ring as this will result in a less effective root system, and eventually a reduced yield.

Once the first trusses of flowers start to set, I begin feeding the plants through the ring with a high potash, liquid fertiliser, doing this once a week until almost the end of its cropping life. Failure to feed regularly

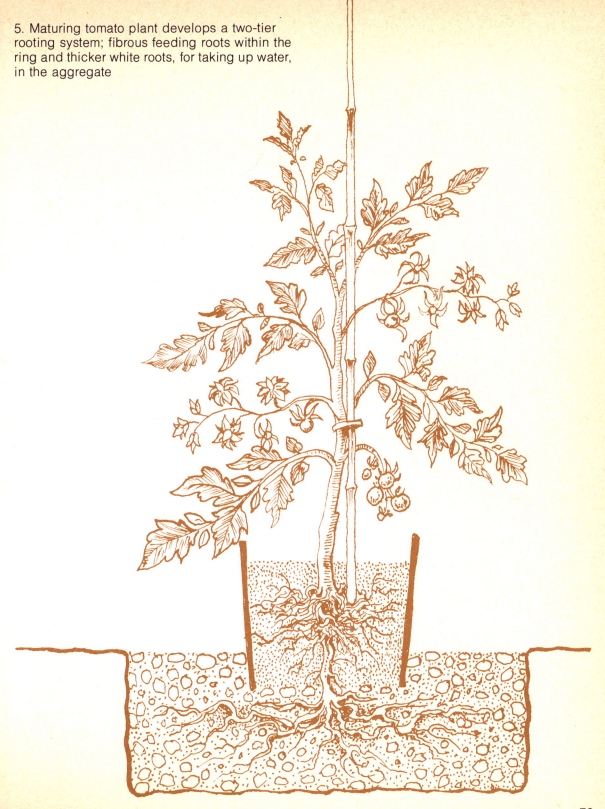

5. Maturing tomato plant develops a two-tier rooting system; fibrous feeding roots within the ring and thicker white roots, for taking up water, in the aggregate

results in a poor set and low yields on the upper trusses.

In a cold unheated greenhouse where planting out must be delayed until the end of May or early June, yields of 4·5 to 6·5 kg (10 to 14 lb) of ripe tomatoes per plant are easily obtainable. In a greenhouse with some heat, earlier planting out is possible and I have had no difficulty in consistently exceeding 9 kg (20 lb) per plant. I find the compact growth habit of Alicante, with its short spaces between the trusses, well suited for ring culture in a small greenhouse.

Growing bags. Another common method of eliminating the problem of soil-borne pests and disease is by using growing bags. At planting out time I like the plants to be actively growing white roots rather than being checked by pot binding. I am convinced that in peat-growing bags two plants per bag yield more fruit than three or four in close competition for light, food and water. Small slits in the sides of the bags provide drainage without any risk of rooting into the soil.

Early in the season plants going into rings or growing bags get away quicker than those in the colder border soil.

Training. For support I use six-ply fillis double, tied to a 38 cm (15 in) wire stake near the plant and to a cross wire above. As the plant grows I encourage it to climb clockwise around the string – this is simpler than using canes.

Growing on a single stem as I do means the removal of every side shoot. The smaller the shoots at the time the better – the removal of large shoots leaves big scars that are open to disease.

Feeding. First truss setting depends on the weather and the conditions within the greenhouse. To ensure a good set I spray each truss of open flowers once with a tomato-fruit setting spray.

Feeding should always start at the set of the first truss. I use a liquid fertiliser with a high potash content, giving a weekly feed which roughly coincides with the succession of trusses.

Watering. Watering can only be judged on the spot. Both over- and underwatering are bad. Shortage of water causes the plant to go limp, and is followed by blossom end rot – dark sunken patches at the flower end of the fruit. Just an hour or two of limpness will do the damage.

Ventilation. Throughout the growing season I have bottom as well as top ventilation, so that the circulation of air is complete. Moist air is essential for good growth and fruit set. During warm weather I water the centre path about midday and close the door for a short while.

Disorders. Starting at the bottom, as the fruit trusses mature I defoliate the stem below the ripe fruit. This improves air circulation immediately, accelerates ripening and reduces the risk of tomato leaf mould – a disease associated with faulty ventilation and cold, damp conditions.

The most common pest problem is whitefly. In the small greenhouse malathion is a practical answer, but spraying must be done weekly as it only kills the adults and not other stages of the whitefly's life cycle.

If tomato flowers drop off at the knuckle it is probably due to a calcium deficiency. I do not wait for this situation to develop but at about the third truss I put a small handful of hydrated lime in a 5-litre (2-gal) bucket and water each plant with it.

At the end of the season the crop tally should be somewhere in the region of 9 kg (20 lb) of fruit per plant, which makes tomato growing a worthwhile hobby.

Growing outdoors. Out of doors, we must remember that we are still dealing with plants that need warmth, moisture and sunshine all the way to do really well. Find a full sun position, if possible sheltered by a wall or fence, with the soil well-prepared but not too

Training tomatoes. Train plants clockwise up a double fillis attached to an overhead cross wire

Remove side shoots as soon as they appear

rich in compost or manure. Over richness leads to excessive growth and slower ripening.

As our summer is short I endeavour to get a few plants out in May and start them off under cloches. This gives a great advantage over plants going out even in the first week of June – the earliest advisable time without cloche protection.

I plant Alicante outside and grow it on a single stem using a strong 1·25-m (4-ft) cane for support. Bush varieties, such as The Amateur, are almost self-supporting.

First truss setting is liable to be indifferent so I spray once with a tomato-fruit-setting spray. Insects should assist adequately with the setting of successive trusses. Feeding is as for indoor tomatoes.

By the beginning of August it is time to stop the plants by pinching out the growing tip. This concentrates all the plants' efforts

Spray open flowers to ensure a good fruit set

into swelling and ripening the four or five trusses being developed.

The removal of leaves below fully-sized fruit trusses speeds ripening. Cut the leaves off cleanly, close to the stem.

Cover plants with thin plastic netting if birds are a nuisance. In September I bring back the cloches to increase the amount of fruit that can be ripened on the plant. Full-sized green fruit will ripen on a windowsill or in a well-ventilated box: our small green ones are made into chutney. Tomatoes outside in pots or boxes will do well but need careful attention to watering.

Sow: February–April under glass
Plant: May–June outside
Harvest: May–October

VARIETIES:
Greenhouse
For all varieties sow February onwards in heat.
Ailsa Craig, well known, still the best for flavour, makes a large plant, subject to greenback.
Alicante, a quality tomato for the small greenhouse, short jointed, heavy cropper, excellent quality.
Eurocross BB, a commercial growers' variety, heavy cropper lacks flavour.
Golden Queen, a yellow tomato full of flavour, sweet, good cropper, needs to be picked as soon as coloured.
Harbinger, smallest tomato, good cropper, excellent quality.
Moneymaker, good-looking tomato, heavy cropper, lacks flavour.
Tangella, a tangerine-coloured tomato, excellent flavour, makes a large plant.
Tigerella, fruit red with golden stripes, excellent flavour, makes a large plant.

Outdoors
Alicante, the variety I grow outside.
The Amateur, a bush type, medium size fruit of good quality.
Sigmabush (F_1 hybrid), bush type of recent introduction, one of the best in a poor season, fruit quality good.

The different shapes of turnips

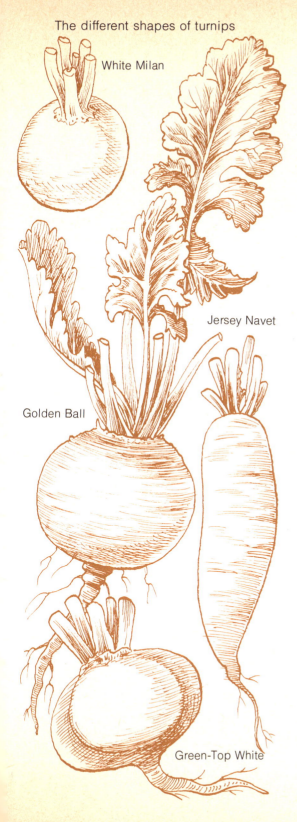

White Milan

Jersey Navet

Golden Ball

Green-Top White

TURNIPS. These are brassicas and so must be fitted into the crop rotation plan accordingly. An early crop may be grown from seed sown in late February or early March in the garden frame. Jersey Navet is a suitable variety.

Turnips are fast growing. From an April sowing outdoors in a sunny place, young turnips would be ready in June. Sow in 1-cm (¾-in) deep drills in a well prepared seedbed that has had a light dressing of hydrated lime.

To prevent flea beetle, when the weather is warm and dry dust the rows with derris just as the seedlings emerge. Thin out to 15 cm (6 in) apart as soon as the seedlings are large enough. This is sufficient spacing as the turnips should be lifted young – they become tough and coarse if they are left until they are large.

White-fleshed varieties are popular – Snowball or White Milan for example – but recently those with golden flesh such as Golden Ball have gained favour on account of their culinary and keeping qualities. Successional sowings every few weeks throughout the summer until early August will give a continuous supply of tender turnips.

Sow: February–August
Distance between plants: 15 cm (6 in)
Distance between rows: 30 cm (12 in)
Harvest: June–November

VARIETIES:
Golden Ball, one of the best for keeping, tender golden flesh, sow June–July.
Green-Top White, white fleshed, often grown to provide turnip tops in the winter and spring, sow late June–July.
Jersey Navet, excellent for sowing early in the year, good flavour.
Snowball, very early, mild, white turnip, sow March to May.
White Milan, a good variety for a very early crop either in cold frame or under cloches, sow February onwards.

Vegetable Growing Calendar

	Jan	Feb	Mar	Apr	May	Jun	Jul	Aug	Sep	Oct	Nov	Dec
Aubergines		G	G				H	H				
Broad beans		O	O	O		H	H	H			O	
Dwarf French beans		G			O	OH	OH	H	H	H		
Runner beans				G	O		H	H	H			
Beetroot				O	O	O	OH	H	H	H		
Sprouting broccoli	H	H	H	O	O		P	P	H	H	H	H
Brussels sprouts	H	H	OH		P	P			H	H	H	
Chinese cabbage							O	H	H	H		
Spring cabbage				H	H		O	O	P			
Summer cabbage		G	O	OP	PH	H						
Red cabbage	H	H		O		P			H	H	H	
Savoy and winter cabbage	H	H	OH	OH	P	P		H	H	H	H	H
Summer and autumn cauliflower			GO	O	O	H	H	H	H	H	H	
Winter cauliflower	H	H	H	OH	OH	P	P					
Kale	H	H	H	OH	O		P				H	H
Carrots	G	G	O	OH	OH	OH	H	H	H	H	G	G
Celery	H	H	G			P			H	H		
Celeriac	H	H		G		P			H	H	H	
Chicory	H	H	H		O	O	O				H	H
Corn salad	H	H						O	O	H	H	H
Courgettes				G	OP	P	H	H	H			
Cucumbers			G			H	H	H	H			
Ridge cucumbers				G	P		H	H	H			
Pickling cucumbers (gherkins)				G	P	P	H	H	H			

Key: G=sow under glass O=sown in open ground P=plant out H=harvest

	Jan	Feb	Mar	Apr	May	Jun	Jul	Aug	Sep	Oct	Nov	Dec
Endive	H	H		O	O	O	O	OH	H	H	H	H
Garlic		P							H			
Kohl rabi				O	O	O	H	H	H	H		
Leeks	H	H	OH			P				H	H	H
Lettuce	GH	GH	GOH	OH	OH	OH	OH	GOH	GOH	OH	OH	OH
Marrows				G	OP	P	H	H	H	H		
Onions	G		OP	OP					H	H		G
Japanese onions						H		O				
Shallots	P	P				H	H					
Spring onions			OH	OH	OH	OH	OH	OH	OH	H		
Parsnips	H	OH	OH								H	H
Peas		O	O	O	OH	OH	OH	H	H	OH	O	
Peppers			G			P	H	H	H			
Pumpkin				G	OP	P			H	H		
Radish		G	OH	OH	OH	OH	OH	H				
Winter radish							O	O	H	H		
Seakale	H	H	P								H	H
Seakale beet				O	O		H	H	H			
Spinach	H	H	OH	O	OH	OH	OH	OH	OH	H	H	H
New Zealand spinach				O	O	H	H	H	H			
Spinach beet	H	H	OH	H		H	OH	H	H	H	H	H
Swede					O					H	H	H
Sweet corn				G	P	P	H	H	H			
Tomatoes		G	G	G	PH	PH	H	H	H	H		
Turnips		O	O	O	O	OH	OH	OH	H	H	H	

Key: G= sow under glass O=sown in open ground P=plant out H=harvest